Land's End

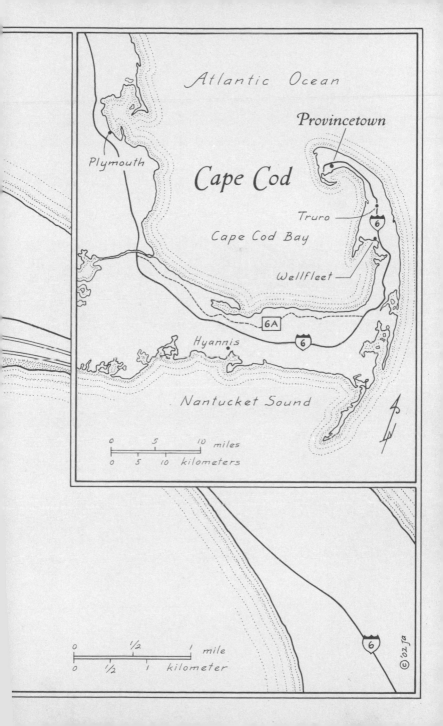

Land's End

A WALK THROUGH PROVINCETOWN

Michael Cunningham

CROWN JOURNEYS

CROWN PUBLISHERS · NEW YORK

917.44
CUN

A list of permission credits appears on page 175.

Copyright © 2002 by Michael Cunningham

All rights reserved. No part of this book may be reproduced or transmitted in any form or by any means, electronic or mechanical, including photocopying, recording, or by any information storage and retrieval system, without permission in writing from the publisher.

Published by Crown Journeys, an imprint of Crown Publishers, New York. Member of the Crown Publishing Group, a division of Random House, Inc. www.randomhouse.com

CROWN JOURNEYS and the Crown Journeys colophon are trademarks of Random House, Inc.

Printed in the United States of America

Design by Lauren Dong
Illustration by John Dowd
Map by Jackie Aher

Library of Congress Cataloging-in-Publication Data

Cunningham, Michael.
    Land's end: a walk through Provincetown/by Michael Cunningham—
1st ed.
    1. Provincetown (Mass.)—Description and travel. 2. Walking—
Massachusetts—Provincetown. 3.Cunningham, Michael. I. Title.
    F74.P96 C86 2002
    917.44'92—dc21

                                                    2002024710

ISBN 0-609-60907-6

10 9 8 7 6 5 4 3 2

First Edition

This book is for Billy Forlenza

Land's End

PROLOGUE

THERE IS A short interval on clear summer evenings in
Provincetown, after the sun has set, when the sky is deep
blue but the hulls of the boats in the harbor retain a last
vestige of light that is visible nowhere else. They become
briefly phosphorescent in a dim blue world. Last summer
as I stood on the beach of the harbor, watching the boats,
I found a coffee cup in the shallows. It's not unusual to
find bits of crockery on this beach (Provincetown's harbor, being shaped like an enormous ladle, catches much
of what the tides stir landward from the waters that sur-
round Cape Cod), but a whole cup is rare. It was not, I'm
sorry to say, the perfect little white china cup that poetry
demands. It was in fact a cheap thing, made in the seventies I suppose, a graceless shallow oval, plastic (hence its
practical but unflattering ability to survive intact), covered
with garish orange and yellow daisies; the official flowers of the insistent, high-gloss optimism I remember from
my adolescence, as talk of revolution dimmed and we all
started, simply, to dance. It wasn't much of a cup, though
it would outlast many of humankind's more vulnerable

attempts to embody the notion of hope in everyday objects. It had gotten onto the beach in one piece, while its lovelier counterparts, concoctions of clay and powdered bone, white as moons, lay in fragments on the ocean floor. This cup contained a prim little clamshell, pewter-colored, with a tiny flourish of violet at its broken hinge, and a scattering of iridescent, mica-ish grit, like tea leaves, at its shallow bottom. I held it up, as if I expected to drink from it, as the boats put out their light.

Land's End

PROVINCETOWN STANDS ON a finger of land at the tip of Cape Cod, the barb at the hook's end, a fragile and low-lying geological assertion that was once knitted together by the roots of trees. Most of the trees, however, were felled by early settlers, and now, with the forests gone, the land on which Provincetown is built is essentially a sandbar, tenuously connected to the mainland, continually reconfigured by the actions of tides. When Thoreau went there in the mid-1800s, he called it "a filmy sliver of land lying flat on the ocean, a mere reflection of a sand-bar on the haze above." It has not changed much since then, at least not when seen from a distance. Built as it is at the very end of the Cape, which unfurls like a genie's shoe from the coastline of Massachusetts, it follows the curve of a long, lazy spiral and looks not out to sea but in, toward the thicker arm of the Cape. The distant lights you see at night across the bay are the neighboring towns of Truro, Wellfleet, and Eastham.

If you stand on the beach on the harbor side, the ocean
proper is behind you. If you turned around, walked diag-
onally through town and across the dunes to the other
side, and sailed east, you'd dock eventually in Lisbon. By
land, the only way back from Provincetown is the way
you've come.

It is by no means inaccessible, but neither is it particularly easy to reach. In the 1700s storms or changes
in currents sometimes washed away the single road that
connected Provincetown to the rest of Cape Cod, and
during those times it was reachable only by boat. Even
when the weather and the ocean permitted, carriages that
negotiated the sandy road often got stuck and sometimes
capsized into the surf. Provincetown is now more firmly
and reliably attached. You can drive there. It's almost
exactly two hours from both Boston and Providence, if
you don't hit traffic, though in summer that's unlikely. You
can fly over from Boston, twenty-five minutes across the
bay, and if you're lucky you might see whales breaching
from the plane. In summer, from mid-May to Columbus
Day, a ferry sails twice a day from Boston. Provincetown
is by nature a destination. It is the land's end; it is not en
route to anywhere else. One of its charms is the fact that
those who go there have made some effort to do so.

Provincetown is three miles long and just slightly more
than two blocks wide. Two streets run its entire length
from east to west: Commercial, a narrow one-way street
where almost all the businesses are, and Bradford, a more
utilitarian two-way street a block north of Commercial.

Residential roads, some of them barely one car wide, run at right angles on a semiregular grid between Commercial and Bradford streets and then, north of Bradford, meander out into dunes or modest hollows of surviving forest, as the terrain dictates. Although the town has been there since before 1720 (the year it was incorporated) and has survived any number of disastrous storms, it is still possible that a major hurricane, if it hit head-on, would simply sweep everything away, since Provincetown has no bedrock, no firm purchase of any kind. It is a city of sand, more or less the way Arctic settlements are cities of ice. A visitor in 1808 wrote to friends in England that the sand was "so light that it drifts about the houses . . . similar to snow in a driving storm. There were no hard surfaces; upon stepping from the houses the foot sinks in the sand." Thoreau noted some forty years later, "The sand is the great enemy here. . . . There was a schoolhouse filled with sand up to the tops of the desks."

The sand has, by now, been domesticated, and Provincetown floats on layers of asphalt, pavement, and brick. Still, any house with a garden has had its soil brought in from elsewhere. Some of the older houses produce their offerings of grass and flowers from earth brought over as ballast in the holds of ships in the 1800s—it is soil that originated in Europe, Asia, or South America. On stormy days gusts of sand still blow through the streets.

*There could be no other town like it. If you were sensi-
tive to crowds, you might expire in summer from human
propinquity. On the other hand, if you were unable to
endure loneliness, the vessel of your person could fill
with dread during the long winter. Martha's Vineyard,
not fifty miles to the south and west, had lived through
the upsurge of mountains and their erosion, through the
rise and fall of oceans, the life and death of great forests
and swamps. Dinosaurs had passed over Martha's Vineyard, and their bones were compacted into the bedrock.
Glaciers had come and gone, sucking the island to
the north, pushing it like a ferry to the south again.
Martha's Vineyard had fossil deposits one million centuries old. The northern reach of Cape Cod, however,
on which my house sat, the land I inhabited—that long
curving spit of shrub and dune that curves in upon itself
in a spiral at the tip of the Cape—had only been formed
by wind and sea over the last ten thousand years. That
cannot amount to more than a night of geological time.*

*Perhaps this is why Provincetown is so beautiful.
Conceived at night (for one would swear it was created
in the course of one dark storm) its sand flats still glis-
tened in the dawn with the moist primeval innocence of*

land exposing itself to the sun for the first time. Decade after decade, artists came to paint the light of Province-town, and comparisons were made to the lagoons of Venice and the marshes of Holland, but then the summer ended and most of the painters left, and the long dingy undergarment of the gray New England winter, gray as the spirit of my mood, came down to visit. One remem-bered then that the land was only ten thousand years old, and one's ghosts had no roots. We did not have old Martha's Vineyard's fossil remains to subdue each spirit, no, there was nothing to domicile our specters who careened with the wind down the two long streets of our town which curved together around the bay like two spinsters on their promenade to church.

NORMAN MAILER,
from *Tough Guys Don't Dance*

The Seasons

*I*N HIGH SUMMER, Provincetown's tourist population is incalculable. In winter it shrinks to just more than 3,800 souls. I find it spectacular in all weathers, but for people looking for a conventional week or two at the beach, it is reliably sunny only in July, August, and early September, and even then days or weeks of rain can blow in from the Atlantic. In summer the days are warm and occasionally hot, the nights almost always cool. In winter it usually snows. Because the town is surrounded by ocean, it never gets as bone-chillingly cold as it does in Boston, twenty-seven miles across the bay.

I grew up in southern California, where the fact that January closely resembles June is generally reckoned a good thing, and a part of my coming of age seems to have involved the development of a low-grade horror of mild weather that pleasantly duplicates itself day after day after day. Provincetown satisfies my appetite for volatility. A curtain of cold rain may sweep through the middle of a sunny summer afternoon, leaving a cooler, clearer version of the same sunshine in its wake. In February a few days of brilliant clarity and relative warmth are not unknown. There are, according to my own private record-keeping, two annual periods of equipoise. There is deep winter, during which a great Arctic curve of frigid quiet obtains. The sky goes as brightly, blankly white as the screen of the drive-in movie theater in Wellfleet. The town is immersed in a low incandescence, as if the light fell not only down from the sky but up from the brown and gray earth as well—from the winter lawns and the silent facades of houses, from the bare branches of trees and the blue-gray bay and the dull pewter of the streets. The air is utterly still; colors are almost violently bright. We who are there then tend to walk the streets carefully, respectfully, as if we feared waking someone. To whatever extent beauty resides in permanence, this is Provincetown at its most beautiful— it seems, in its winter slumber, to be revealed in its actual state, without its jewelry or feathers, like a white marble queen; a woman who, in life, may have been irritable and erratic, prone to sulks, too easily cheered by velvets and brocades; now asleep forever in a cathedral close, her eyes peacefully shut, her face arranged in an expression of mournful bemusement as the living flit by with their cameras and candles, their little prayers.

Then there is the heart of summer, which occurs sometime on or before the middle of August. Province-town is far north, nearer to Nova Scotia than it is to Florida—fall comes early there. By Labor Day some of the leaves are already showing hints of red and yellow at their edges. But during the second week of August (sometimes earlier, sometimes later), there is a deep blue bowl of perfect days, noisier than winter but possessed of a similar underlying silence; a similar sense that the world is and will always be just this way—calm and warm, bleached with brightness, its contrasts subdued by a shimmer that makes it difficult to determine precisely where the ocean ends and the sky begins. One August afternoon several years ago I was reading on a pier and felt, suddenly, that I was in the middle of an enormous clock and that it was, at that moment, precisely noon; that I was present for the exact middle of the vernal year. A minute before it had still been rising summer; a minute later summer's decline would start, though nothing would appear to have changed.

I love these periods of stillness, look forward to them, though the weather is most wonderful, to me, in late spring and early fall. May and June in Provincetown tend to mists and fogs, and the town is as greenly muted as a village in the Scottish highlands. The foghorn blows all day as well as all night. The town has opened for the summer—stores and restaurants are lit, the single surviving movie theater is back in business—but few tourists have arrived yet. The town is made up, for these weeks, almost entirely of its year-round and its full-time summer population, the people who work in the stores and restaurants, and they walk on Commercial Street through the mist exclaiming over one another, inquiring about how the winter went, full of a buoyancy that will erode steadily away until it reaches the point of exhaustion and exasperation that arrives on or near Labor Day weekend. But for now, during these weeks, there's all that sex and dancing ahead; there's all that money to be made. Hundreds of thousands of strangers are on their way—anyone could fall in love. There's a low spark, a hazy green glow, all the more potent for the drizzle that pervades. At this time of year you might stroll down Commercial Street after midnight, when the streetlamps illuminate little more than circles of fog, and find yourself entirely alone save for the foraging skunks; a man named Butchy, who wears a blue motorcycle helmet and a chest-length beard, and wanders the streets at night with a black plastic trash bag full of something; and another man in a blond wig and a silver lamé dress, walking unaccompanied twenty paces ahead, singing "Loving You" like a crackpot Lorelei, still trying to lure sailors to their deaths though she's no longer what she was.

In fall, from mid-September through the end of October, the opposite process occurs. Fall is probably never so thoroughly suffused with its piquant, precarious beauty as it is in a town about to go to sleep for the winter. The lights are blinking out, one by one: first the movie theater closes, then some of the more ephemeral boutiques. Every week brings more absences. Still, most of the businesses hang on until Columbus Day weekend, but after that the town is in winter mode. It's much more a year-round proposition than it was when I arrived there twenty years ago—a fair number of places open on weekends through New Year's Day, and some open again as early as April; there are now two good year-round bookshops and a record store—but by mid-January there will be only a handful of bars, a restaurant or two, and a scattering of shops. By February you could walk down Commercial Street late on a weekday night and pass no one at all. Snow blows down from the rooftops, eddies, and glints in the empty streetlight.

But from Labor Day through Halloween, the place is almost unbearably beautiful. The air during these weeks seems less like ether and more like a semisolid, clear and yet dense somehow, as if it were filled with the finest imaginable golden pollen. The sky tends toward brilliant ice-blue, and every thing and being is invested with a soft, gold-ish glow. Tin cans look good in this light; discarded shopping bags do. I'm not poet enough to tell you what the salt marsh looks like at high tide. I confess that when I lived year-round in Provincetown, I tended to become irritable toward the end of October, when one supernal day after another seemed to imply that the only reasonable human act was to abandon your foolish errands and plans, go outside, and fall to your knees. I found myself looking forward to the relative drear of November, when the light whitened and the streets became papered with dead leaves; when cans and shopping bags looked like simple trash again. At least by November I could get some work done.

My First Time

I FIRST CAME to Provincetown twenty years ago, in a state of such deep embarrassment I could no longer imagine myself without it. I was twenty-eight. I had just finished two years at the Writers' Workshop at the University of Iowa and had been offered a residency at the Fine Arts Work Center in Provincetown, which awards seven-month fellowships, from October to May, to a small body of writers and visual artists, who are each given a studio apartment, a monthly stipend, and a full, uninterrupted span of time in which to work. It is a remarkable act of beneficence. For me it felt like nothing short of rescue, since I had ended my two years in Iowa with no money and no prospects.

Still, I felt old in a way only the young can feel. I would be thirty soon and had not attained anything even my mother could bring herself to call success. Before going to graduate school, I had wandered around the West, getting odd jobs, trying to write. I had published a couple of short stories and begun several novels, the kind young men tend to write, meant to teach the reading public a lesson or two about how to live. Each time I'd realized that I had no idea how people should live, abandoned the book in question, and started another. I was furious and full of shame. I could, for the first time, imagine myself a failure.

Before I applied for the fellowship, I had never heard of Provincetown. I had never been east of Chicago. I drove there with my cartons of books and clothes, accompanied by two friends from graduate school who lived in Providence, Rhode Island. As we drove in their van down Commercial Street, my friend Sarah put her hands over her eyes and said, "God, it's like the set of *The Cabinet of Dr. Caligari*." Sarah was prone to hyperbole (we all were), but I couldn't disagree with her. I had pictured a small New England town like the ones I'd seen in movies. I had expected prim white saltboxes with well-tended gardens, a modest white church surrounded by modest old tombstones, and a central square of some sort with a white bandstand quietly fading on a square of bright green lawn.

Instead I found Commercial Street, which curves as it runs its course from east to west, so there's no horizon line—as you drive along, the street closes off behind you and ahead of you. Most of the houses and shops front right up on the narrow sidewalk, standing shoulder to shoulder. The stores, generally, are serviceable clapboard buildings, unornamented, innocent of the cupolas and widows' walks I'd expected before I came. There were, on that day in late September, many signs advertising end-of-season sales, and occasional strings of colored pennants like the ones strung over used-car lots. The stores all looked slightly smaller than life size, the way the buildings on Main Street USA in Disneyland are built at eleven inches to the foot, so as to appear less inhibiting than real buildings in an actual town, though the effect here, at least on me, was not at all comforting. The ocean was nowhere in sight. The people we passed were not the prosperous, slightly hippie-fied citizens I'd expected. They were mostly tourists, pushing children in strollers past the souvenir shops. They looked generally as baffled and disappointed as we were.

I moved into my studio and said good-bye to Sarah and Jamie the way a child says good-bye to his parents as they leave him at a doubtful-looking summer camp. It was late afternoon, just beginning to get dark. I went off to explore the town.

On foot the initial signs were more encouraging than they'd been from Sarah and Jamie's van. I learned that if you found your way down among the buildings, you soon reached the bay, a vast body of dark blue water where a foghorn blew like a bassoon and where, as evening progressed, a single green light, like the one Gatsby worshiped, shone on a peninsula several hundred yards out. I discovered a movie theater in the center of town, a stalwart red-brick building in the tradition of small-town American movie palaces (it has since burned down), which was showing *Gone With the Wind*. The show started in twenty minutes. I saw *Gone With the Wind* among five or six other patrons, and it was thoroughly satisfying, even if the print was rather old and patched together, so that when Scarlett O'Hara stumbled on the landing in her Atlanta mansion, she was teleported instantaneously to the bottom of the stairs.

When I left the theater, however, I learned that it was screening *Gone With the Wind* one more time, the following night, and then closing until May. The other two theaters had already closed for the season. All right, I thought. Who needs movies? I'll read every night. I walked on and found a nice little bar where lean women in leather jackets played pool and a covey of men sat by the fireplace, laughing at jokes so familiar they barely needed to be told at all. I ordered a beer and learned from the bartender that the bar would be open until the end of the week and would then close until May.

Over the next few days it became apparent that the entire town, with the exception of essentials like the grocery and drug stores and, bless it, a courageous little bookshop, intended to close from early October until mid-May. There would be fewer and fewer tourists. There would soon be only, as I quickly learned, the handful of local residents, bundled against the increasingly cold weather, most of them vanished by nightfall except the town's most visible disturbed person, a handsome, disheveled man who looked slightly scorched, as if he had just escaped from a fire, and who walked up and down Commercial Street all day and into the night, in the same dark jeans and flannel shirt, muttering ferociously into the gelid air. There would be two bars, both of which catered to fishermen, and one struggling vegetarian café. All right, I thought. No distractions. I'll just write and read for seven months.

I did read, though restlessly and randomly—half of *The Charterhouse of Parma,* some Philip Roth, some Dorothy Sayers. I had trouble concentrating. I did not write, although I tried my hardest to. My bluff had been called. Given the ideal circumstances, a room of my own, free of distractions, I found I could not write at all. I stayed up late and slept as late as I could, but I had to wake eventually and face another empty day during which I would stare at my typewriter, put down and cross out a sentence or two, then walk along the bay and the empty street, past the boarded-up souvenir shops and the muttering man, until it was night and I could make dinner, start drinking, and read, or try to read. I bought an old black-and-white television set and watched it for hours and hours, with an addict's hopeless pleasure, derived in part from my own willingness to let things slide. That winter I lost not only what felt like my last hold on optimism but my belief in optimism itself. At the end of my twenties, I believed I was being given an early tour of the old age home, one endless day followed by another, sleep the only conceivable reward. On one particularly bleak night in February, I sat on my scratchy plaid sofabed with a vodka in my hand, rocking slightly as the television droned, and promised that if I survived the next few months, I would leave Provincetown and not only never return but never again go to any human settlement with a population under one million.

And somehow, in the end, I fell in love with Provincetown, the way you might meet someone you consider strange, irritating, potentially dangerous but whom, eventually, you find yourself marrying. I stayed for the summer, after my fellowship ran out, working in a bar—I had once again gotten myself to a remote place with no money and no obvious next move. I went to New York in the fall, liked New York, but found to my surprise that I missed Provincetown, against my will, the way you begin to recognize the early symptoms of love or the flu. Certain images had taken up particularly stubborn residence in my mind. There had been a moment in mid-December, at dusk, at the far west end of town, where the street dead-ends at a salt marsh and curves back on itself, attended only by an illuminated telephone booth, a perfect box of wan yellow light against the black-green marsh and the purpled sky. I had stood and watched that rectangle of light and the marsh behind it as if they contained some beauty too final and bleak to articulate. A month or so later I had watched a great silver barge of a nocturnal cloud moving serenely across the frozen stars as I stood shivering at the end of a pier, trying and failing to cry, staring at the green light on Long Point and hearing the foghorn blow its bassoon note over and over again—come home, child, the ice mother is waiting for you, and she doesn't need you to strive or accomplish, she only wants you to sleep. Provincetown had offered its demonstrations of frigid, off-season grandeur, and then it had offered the spring thaw, when people began to appear on the streets again, more of them every weekend. The salty silence dissipated; smells of popcorn and fried food stirred themselves up. Music sifted out of the bars, and the town began to fill with the possibility of sex. I took all that with me to New York. As I walked the streets of New York, I began to wonder if, for the first time in my life, I had been reduced that winter to so little that I could see the dreadful, rock-hard opulence of the world, that which remains when idealism and sentimentality have fallen away. Provincetown in its winter desolation and its subsequent, temporary revival came to seem more real, or at least more trustworthy, than any other place I'd ever been. It began to feel (though I'd never have used this word then) like home.

I went back the following summer, telling myself I was going only to make money and have sex. I fell in love with a handsome, highly dramatic man who owned a café on the East End. I insisted I couldn't ever live in Provincetown again, but ultimately moved there to live with him. Several years later I left him but kept coming back to the town.

Now I go there every chance I get. Kenny, the man with whom I live, and I have bought a house on the East End. If I die tomorrow, Provincetown is where I'd want my ashes scattered. Who knows why we fall in love, with places or people, with objects or ideas? Thirty centuries of literature haven't begun to solve the mystery; nor have they in any way slaked our interest in it.

Provincetown is a mysterious place, and those of us who love it tend to do so with a peculiar, inscrutable intensity. With this book I hope to offer neither more nor less than the story of my own particular devotion, with the understanding that my Provincetown differs profoundly from the Provincetown of others. It is not a place that inspires objectivity—even its history is as much speculation and rumor as it is recorded fact—and the Provincetown you get from me, aside from certain particulars of geography and weather, will not resemble the Provincetown you would get from the head librarian, from the native-born fisherman who still struggles to make a living from the depleted waters of the North Atlantic, or from the woman who moved there twenty years ago to live as much apart from men as she possibly could. This book is a little plastic cup with a clamshell in it, found in the tidal shallows, raised in slightly bewildered homage as the boats in the harbor shine like ghosts.

LONG POINT LIGHT

Long Point's apparitional
this warm spring morning,
the strand a blur of sandy light,

and the square white
of the lighthouse—separated from us
by the bay's ultramarine

as if it were nowhere
we could ever go—gleams
like a tower's ghost, hazing

into the rinsed blue of March,
our last outpost in the huge
indetermination of sea.

It seems cheerful enough,
in the strengthening sunlight,
fixed point accompanying our walk

along the shore. Sometimes I think
it's the where-we-will-be,
only not yet, like some visible outcropping

of the afterlife. In the dark
    its deeper invitations emerge:
        green witness at night's end,

flickering margin of horizon,
    marker of safety and limit.
        But limitless, the way it calls us,

and where it seems to want us
    to come. And so I invite it
        into the poem, to speak,

and the lighthouse says:
    Here is the world you asked for,
        gorgeous and opportune,

here is nine o'clock harbor-wide,
    and a glinting code: promise and warning.
        The morning's the size of heaven.

What will you do with it?

MARK DOTY

Wilderness

ALTHOUGH THE DESKS in the schools are no longer half buried in sand, and sand-drifts no longer pile up against the walls of houses, Provincetown is still thoroughly infiltrated by its skittish, sandy wilderness. Auto body shops stand in the shadows of dunes; the waterfront houses are built directly on sand and have shells and beach grass where their inland sisters would have lawns. There is no place where you can't hear the foghorn. The wilderness offers escape from the noise and commerce; town offers at least partial sanctuary from the abiding patience out there, that which sifts through your windows at night and will be there long after you are gone.

In a sense Provincetown *is* a beach. If you stand on the shore watching the tide recede, you are merely that much closer to the water and that much more available to weather than you would be in the middle of town. All along the bay side, the entire length of town, the beach slopes gently, bearded with kelp and dry sea grass. Because

Provincetown stands low on the continental shelf, it is profoundly affected by tides, which can exceed a twelve-foot drop at the syzygy of sun, moon, and earth. Interludes of beach that are more than a hundred yards wide at low tide vanish entirely when the tide is high. The water of the bay is utterly calm in most weathers and warmer than that of the ocean beaches, but this being the North Atlantic, no water anywhere is ever what you could rightfully call warm, not even in August. Except in extreme weather the bay beach is entirely domesticated, the backyard of the town, never empty but never crowded, either; there is no surf there, and the water that laps docilely up against the shore is always full of boats. The bay beach is especially good for dogs and small children, whose only other access to large, untrammeled space is the playing field of the high school on the hill. The bay beach is also good for strolling along in solitude, which is most satisfying, to me, on clear winter days, when the air is almost painfully sharp and scraps of snow linger on the sand. The beach is strewn with shells, but they are New England shells, almost exclusively bivalves, running from gray to brown to lighter brown with minor hints of mauve or deep, dusty purple. This is not a marine landscape prone to pinks or pale blues. The beach does yield the occasional treasure, an old clay pipe or a whole glass bottle that the ocean has turned opalescent. Paul Bowen, a sculptor who combs the beaches incessantly, has even found a few porcelain dolls' heads, arms, and legs over the years, and I always walk along that section hoping to see a tiny white face, half buried in sand, offering prim scarlet lips and one empty blue eye from among the stones and shards.

LONG POINT

The remotest end of the sandy spiral on which Provincetown stands—the very tip of the Cape's languidly unfurling hook—is called Long Point, a narrow scrap of dunes and grass. It is tentatively part of the mainland, but centuries ago the ocean dissolved most of the scrawny neck of sand that connected it. There is now a jetty that attaches Long Point to the far West End, built in 1911. In the 1700s, though, when Long Point was essentially an island, a community started up there, and eventually it grew to about two hundred people, most of whom operated salt works, where sea water was evaporated for salt. Everything these citizens needed, everything the Atlantic didn't provide, was brought over by boat from Provincetown proper.

During the War of 1812 the British occupied Provincetown and cut off supplies to the people on Long Point. When the Civil War broke out, the people of Provincetown, fearing that the Confederate Army would invade and set up a similar blockade, built two fortresses of sand on Long Point, with a cannon in each. The Confederates never came anywhere near Provincetown, however, and as volunteers stood guard day after day and night after night over an uncontested stretch of salt water, the fortresses came to be known as Fort Useless and Fort Ridiculous.

Before the Civil War, toward the middle of the 1800s, the citizens of Long Point began to feel that they'd made a mistake in settling there at all. Their houses were almost flirtatiously available to gales and hurricanes, their salt wasn't selling as it once had, and the notion that every egg, darning needle, or pair of socks had to be ordered and delivered by boat had lost its charm. So they had their houses, forty-eight of them, jacked up, loaded onto barges, and floated over to the mainland. Most of the old houses in Provincetown, being built on sand, had no foundations at all and could be moved from one place to another without much more difficulty than what would be involved in transporting a drydocked boat across land. On the mainland houses perched at the tops of dunes were known sometimes to work their way down slowly, over the years, until they rested at the feet of the dunes they had once crested.

The houses that were floated over from Long Point still stand, mostly in the West End of Provincetown, though there are a few in the East End as well. Each of them bears a blue plaque, with a picture of a house on a barge floating calmly over white squiggles of unprotesting waves.

At the tide's lowest point you can walk to Long Point from the West End, over the expanse of wet sand. You can walk there, regardless of the tides, across the jetty that starts at the far west end of Commercial Street. The jetty is a thirty-foot-wide ribbon of rough granite blocks that extends almost to its own vanishing point when you stand on the mainland looking out to Long Point. You may want to walk all the way to the point, or you may just want to go partway out and sit on the rocks for a while. In summer, an hour or so before high tide, when the water is moving in, you can slide in from the rocks and let yourself be carried along by the tide, almost all the way back to shore.

If you do walk to Long Point, you will find yourself on a spit of sand about three hundred yards wide, with bay beach on one side, ocean beach on the other, and a swatch of dune grass running down the middle. It sports, like an austere ornament, a lighthouse and a long-empty shed once used to store oil for the light. You will be almost alone there, though the water around you will be thoroughly populated by boats. It is a favorite nesting ground for terns and gulls. When I went out there years ago with Christy, the man with whom I lived then, he strode into the dune grass and stirred up the birds. If I tell you that he stood exultantly among hundreds of shrieking white birds that circled and swooped furiously around him, looking just like a figure out of Dante, grinning majestically, while I stood by and worried about what it was doing to the birds, you may know everything you need to know about why we were together and why we had to part.

THE SALT MARSH

Just beyond the jetty, past the hairpin curve Commercial Street makes as it turns back on itself and changes its name to Bradford Street, is the salt marsh. The long road that starts at the landward end of Cape Cod ends here, at this wild lawn of sea grass. The marsh reliably tells the time, the state of the weather, and the season: emerald in spring and summer, gold in fall, various browns in winter. Wind when it blows raises flashes and swells of paler color among the grasses and reeds, so you can stand at the edge of the marsh and see just how strongly the wind is blowing, and in what direction. Because the marsh is always at least partly flooded, reflected sky lights the grass from below. On sunny days it can seem unnaturally bright, and on cloudy days it looks even brighter.

It is puddled during low tides, inundated when the tide is high. It terminates in a range of dunes, beyond which is the ocean, though you can't see it from where you now stand. You may see a heron or two, wading among the tidal pools. You will assuredly see the little white thumb of Wood End lighthouse, far away. (It is not the one on Long Point.) I've never gone there and don't intend to. I know—or rather, I can imagine—that up close it's merely an old plaster tower, its paint cracked and peeling, spattered all over its concrete base with seagull shit. I prefer that it remain a distant object, its romance undiluted, an image out of Virginia Woolf. I believe every city and town should contain at least one remote spot, preferably a beautiful and mysterious one, that you see but never visit.

HERRING COVE

Herring Cove is one of Provincetown's two official public beaches. The other is Race Point. Herring Cove is the nearer of the two to town—you can walk or bike there.

In summer, the town loop bus will take you there for free. From the salt marsh it's about a half mile to the official public entrance, with its parking lot and snack bar, but my preferred point of ingress is the nearer one, across the dunes.

Go north from the salt marsh, past a small, murky lagoon to the right of the road, into a stand of trees, and stop where you see all the bicycles parked. There's an unambiguous entrance there, between the trees.

It takes about fifteen minutes to get to the beach. You will find yourself in tidal flats, with high dunes on either side and the curving wall of dunes that line the ocean straight ahead. You may see the masts and upper deck of a boat sailing by, and that is a good if slightly surreal sight, a half-boat skimming placidly along over the sand.

There is a vague but discernible path, and you should stay on it. The landscape is fragile—it does not respond well to footsteps. If you're walking out at low tide, the sand will be mostly dry, dotted here and there with clear pools. If you're walking out at high tide, you will have to wade. If you go there in late afternoon or early evening, the dunes will glow with a pink-orange light like the inside of a conch shell.

The tidal pools, if it's medium or high tide, will be full of minnows and little blue-black crabs. It is possible, though very rare, to see schools of squid that have gotten trapped by the receding tide and are waiting for the ocean to return. Squid alive are nothing like the ones in fish markets. They go opaque when they die. Alive, they are translucent, like jellyfish, and their eyes, though utterly unmammalian, are pale blue. When they swim, you see their eyes most clearly, and the spark of their tentacles.

Because this terrain is periodically submerged, you'll find a good deal of what the ocean contains as you go along. The path is strewn with the bodies of crabs, which bleach to a freckled salmon color that they do not possess in life and ultimately to alabaster. You may see a dead bass or two, in the process of being picked clean by the gulls. You will see kelp and driftwood, sometimes in considerable piles, and you will see strands of rope torn from fishermen's nets, black or yellow or turquoise or orange. I once found the end of a seagull's wing out there, a harp of white feathers, and took it home to Kenny, glad not only to have happened upon such a thing but to be a man carrying a wing home to his lover, who would not be repelled by its gruesome beauty.

This walk, and the beach it leads to, is largely the province of gay men. As you near the beach and the dunes dwindle down into a broad, shallow basin, you'll pass paths that meander out into the grass. They are dry at low tide. At high tide the water is as high as a man's waist. These paths, this whole arena, is thoroughly populated on summer days—it is the Piazza San Marco of gay male Provincetown. Men walk to and from the beach. Men browse among the dunes, lounge on the small temporary islands that stand among the pools when the tide is in, wade or swim in the deeper parts. The paths that snake through the tall grasses form an elaborate series of mazes, and if you follow the paths at medium to high tide, you will find yourself up to your knees or waist in gently moving water surrounded on both sides by hedges of high grass. Men go into the grasses to have sex, and if you are uninterested in having sex with strangers or are bothered by the sight of other people doing it, you should avoid the grass maze and proceed directly to the beach, though even if you eschew the remoter reaches, you might pass two or more men sporting together, out in the open. In this bright, tidal landscape the men having sex always seem, at least to me, innocently bacchanalian—more creaturely than lewd. They seem to belong to a different version of the world, a more sylvan and semiclassical one, shameless and wild. They seem to have been freed from their labors and sorrows, their fears, even their hopes, and been given a summer hour or two in which desire is all that matters. I would be happy if the men who have sex in the salt marsh could be persuaded to wear fur leggings with hooves over their feet, attach little nubs of horns to their foreheads, and blow wistful tunes on pipes as they wander through the labyrinths of grass and water.

When you climb over the dunes that front on the ocean, you arrive at the beach, where the water is almost always calm, since Herring Cove lies on the inward curl of the Cape and faces southwest rather than east. By international standards Herring Cove is not much of a beach. It is relatively narrow, and the sand near the water is almost entirely covered with stones that are difficult to walk on. New England, even at its most sybaritic, usually involves some measure of challenge or inconvenience; it is not prone to dropping ripe fruit straight from the tree into your outstretched hand. The stones themselves are lovely, for whatever comfort that may offer. They are consistently smooth and oval, shaped by the water—the most symmetrical of them are like Noguchi sculptures. If you are inclined to pick up stones from the beach, I should warn you that many of them, when wet, appear to be fantastic shades of ochre or deep red or dark green, but they lose their color after they dry. I prefer the glossy black ones, which dry to various shades of gray, from yellow-gray to a satisfying milky gray like chalk erased from a blackboard. I keep a bowl of them on my desk.

The southern part of the beach, in summer, is full of men. You will see almost no one there who is not a man. Men lie on the sand in groups, talking and laughing, listening to music. They promenade, wearing very little, and some of them are beautiful, though the whole notion of strolling lithely and muscularly along the sand, looking to populate strangers' dreams, is complicated by the stones, which effectively eliminate the possibility of maintaining regal composure for more than a few paces at a time. The whole business of cruising and being cruised at Herring Cove is a slightly comic one, very different from, say, the broad sandy highway of a beach at Fire Island, where ambitious objects of desire can saunter from east to west and back again as imperturbably as floats in a military parade.

If you walk along the beach to your left, you'll get, eventually, to the Wood End lighthouse and, ultimately, out to Long Point. If you walk to your right, you'll reach the beach's official entrance, where the parking lot is. Close to the entrance is the women's section.

The transformation is fairly abrupt. For some time you will have walked among men lying on towels (with a few of the braver specimens splashing around in the chilly water); then you will pass through a short intermediate strip of men mixed with women; and then the beach will be full, almost exclusively, of women.

It is considered a truism in Provincetown that gay men go to the beach with Speedos and a towel, while lesbians take as much as they can carry. One resists generalities (and is attracted to generalities), but it is undeniable that here, in the women's section, you are much more likely to see folding beach chairs, umbrellas, coolers, inflatable rafts, rubber sandals for walking over the stones, and other appurtenances. The women arrayed on the sand here are, to roughly equal extents, domestic and Amazonian. As a man walking through their sector, I always feel that I'm in a foreign country—a Sapphic society every bit as strange and fabulous, and just as particular unto itself, as the tribes of satyrs roaming the watery paths in the dunes. Bare breasts are more the norm than the exception here, and for some of us it is a unique opportunity to understand that the female breast is among the more profoundly variable of human wonders. Here are women with breasts firm as pears. Here are women whose breasts are mere pale rises of flesh, more modest by far than the pectorals of most of the men lounging and romping just up the beach, with pert and defiant cantaloupe-colored nipples the size of fingertips. Here are women with majestic moons, tropically pink, marbled by traceries of blue-green veins, topped with low-lying, elliptical aureoles of creamy brown. The women in the women's section are more likely than the men to be throwing balls or Frisbees at the water's edge. They are more likely to be swimming with dogs. They are far more likely to have children, who are entirely absent in the men's section. The women's part of the beach is a welter of children, of all races, and there are more of them every year.

If you continue on, you will pass an unfortunate asphalt embankment—atop it is a snack bar, bathrooms, and showers. Farther still you will find yourself on a long stretch of beach dominated by straight families who have parked their campers or trailers and more or less settled in. Some of the campers and trailers have awnings, where grandparents sit in the shade admiring the view or reading or tending to barbecue grills. Men and women fish from the beach and often wait for a strike sitting on aluminum lawn chairs. Kids run all over the place. The people on this part of the beach are noisier, less sexual, more communal. The gay and lesbian sections are, to a certain extent, feudal—each encampment of friends and lovers and children and pets tends to regard only itself, to speak only to acquaintances as they pass, and to observe strangers either surreptitiously or not at all. While I'm certain that these straight families don't know each other and probably don't mingle, they require so much more space, with their campers and barbecues and fishing gear, their three or four generations, that turf lines are impossible to maintain. Compared with the gay men and lesbians up the beach, they are differently yoked into their lives. They are ostentatiously available to their spouses and parents and children, and so, to an outsider anyway, they seem more like a village, with all that villages imply about common purpose. It seems—though I don't imagine this is literally true—that one mother will casually pluck another woman's child from the surf, and that one grandfather will offhandedly flip the burgers of another man's son as the two middle-aged boys in question reel in a bluefish.

Farther down the beach is Hatches Harbor, one of the lesser-known wonders of Provincetown.

Hatches Harbor

Although I am agnostic on the subjects of magic, earth spirits, and conscious but invisible forces, I can't deny that several places in Provincetown possess some sort of power beyond their physical attributes. Hatches Harbor is one such place. It is some distance beyond the public beach, well past the outer reaches of the parking lot, so the only way to get there is by walking on the sand. It is, as its name implies, a natural harbor, a vulnerable point in the land mass where the ocean has curled its way in. It was once an estuary that extended inland for over a mile, but a dike built in the 1930s reduced it to a series of braided tidal channels.

Hatches Harbor is not well known. You are likely to find, at most, a few other people there, and you are at least as likely to be entirely alone. The harbor is dominated by an enormous sandbar that stretches across it like the broad back of a whale, albeit the placid, utterly smooth whale's back you might find in a children's book. To the north stands still another lighthouse, bigger than the other two in Provincetown, a serious lighthouse, tall and staunch, neither sweet nor toylike as the other two are, meant to warn big ships of true dangers. (Over the centuries at least a hundred ships have sunk in these waters.) Inland, directly behind you as you face the ocean, are dunes and scrub pine. None of this is especially dramatic or spectacular, not in the way of Delphi or the Oregon coast. Surf doesn't crash against cliffs here, eagles don't wheel in the sky. It has a spare and subtle beauty, more nearly related to parts of the New Mexico desert or the lakes of Finland. The harbor, the horizon, and the dunes are all in perfect proportion, visibly part of the same overarching idea. It has a way of gently insisting on the beauty of the small— look here, three round stones in a round cup of clear water. Like any proper mystery, it can't be adequately described or explained. I can only tell you that it is a place of great tranquillity, and that if you go there and stay for an hour or longer, you may feel, when you walk back, that you've been farther and longer away than you have actually been.

THE DUNES

Behind the beach at Herring Cove, behind all of Provincetown, is the Cape Cod National Seashore, established during the Kennedy administration as a recreation area and nature preserve. Whatever our feelings about John F. Kennedy as president, we can be grateful to him for that. The town cannot expand past a certain point; no one can build a resort hotel in the dunes or on the ocean beaches. The dunes are an intact ecosystem, as particular unto themselves as Zion in Utah or the Florida Everglades, though unlike Zion or the Everglades they were formed, in part, by man. Early settlers felled the trees for fuel and lumber, and replanted the landscape with pitch pine and scrub oak. With the big trees gone, a sand-sea began working its methodical way in from the beaches, and what you are seeing in this sedate landscape is actually an ongoing process of erosion.

The best way to go through the dunes is on a bicycle, which you can rent from one of four places in town. A single snake of trail, not conspicuously marked, starts from the far end of the parking lot at Herring Cove and winds through the dunes. The dunescape is simultaneously verdant and lunar. It is dotted with brush and scrubby, stunted pine. It has a smell: pine and salt, with an undercurrent of something I can only describe as dusty and green. In patches the landscape is almost pure sand, pristine as sugar. The sandy areas seem primeval in their silence and shadows, though they are, of course, not ancient at all—they weren't like this a hundred years ago; a century from now they will be visibly different. Still, I often feel when I'm out there that I'm palpably on the surface of a planet, with a thin illusion of blue overhead and the universe beyond. It is especially wonderful to ride through the dunes at night, when the moon is full.

In these same dunes but miles up Cape, too far for biking, is the place where Guglielmo Marconi first tested the telegraph—where a human being was able, for the first time, to send and receive wireless messages across the Atlantic. The building in which he conducted his experiment has since fallen into the ocean, but a weathered gazebo bearing a plaque stands today to commemorate the spot where, over a hundred years ago, Marconi sat day after day and night after night, convinced that he could communicate not only with those living on other continents but with the dead as well. He thought sound waves did not vanish over time; he believed he could find a way to hear the cries of men on ships sunk long ago, the voices of children whose own children were ancient by then, the musket reports of Columbus's men as they showed the Tecumwah tribe what terrible new gods had arrived on their shores.

The Marconi Station, however, is a separate trip altogether, one that would require a car. This trail you're on is merely a meandering, four-mile-long circle that takes you back, ultimately, to the East End of Provincetown. It offers only one choice, at roughly its midpoint. You can go straight ahead, through the beech forest and ultimately back to town, or you can turn left and ride out to Race Point.

RACE POINT

The beach at Race Point is, to my mind, superior to the one at Herring Cove, and I, who enjoy a beach full of gay men, have often wished my brothers had elected to colonize Race Point instead. Its sole disadvantage is the fact that it is several miles from town, and you can get there only on a bicycle or in a car. If you drive, you may very well find the parking lot full by ten A.M. on a summer day.

The beach at Race Point arcs north to northwest. It is more directly canted toward the open ocean than the one at Herring Cove, and so the water there is prone to do something more exciting than just plash quietly up against the sand. It has actual waves, though you'd have to go farther still, to the beaches of Truro and Wellfleet, before encountering anything that could be called surf. To get to the beach, you lope down a bank of dunes, on which patches of low grass have drawn windblown circles around themselves in the sand. The beach is broad and generous, at all tides, and not nearly so strewn with stones. Being less accessible, it is never as crowded as the beach at Herring Cove, and the people who go there are much more a mixed bag. You'll find yourself among tourist families, townies with or without families, and the occasional renegade gay man or lesbian. It was at Race Point, several years ago, that we encountered a lesson in the mutability of desire, courtesy of Uncle Donald.

Kenny and I had gone with our friend Melanie to Race Point on an August afternoon (Melanie has a car) and put down our towels near a small family gathering. Beaches are, of course, perfect sites for eavesdropping, and as we lay in the sun, we quickly discerned the following about our neighbors. They were a handsome, dark-haired Englishwoman, her American husband, their five-year-old son, and the woman's gay younger brother, Donald. We knew his name was Donald because the little boy, transported by love, said "Uncle Donald" whenever it was called for and sometimes when it was not. Uncle Donald was a lithe man in his early thirties, wearing blue Speedos. He was wonderful with the child. They played together in the water, played in the sand; Uncle Donald was patient if ironic about the child's endless assertion of suddenly devised games with arcane and elaborate rules. When Uncle Donald reached his limit, they lay down together on his towel. The boy announced that Uncle Donald was his mattress, sprawled on top of him, and fell asleep. Uncle Donald teased his sister, who teased him back. The phrase "looking for love in all the wrong places" was mentioned. In repose, with a slumbering child on his stomach, Donald might have been carved from pale pink marble. His lean, compact body was hairless except for two light-brown tufts in his armpits. His face, in profile, was angular, with a potent brow and a firm jut of chin. Kenny and I agreed, in whispers, that we wanted him and wanted, with roughly equivalent ardor, to *be* him.

Melanie declared her willingness to give up women, at least for a while. Donald was wry and kind; innocently virtuous the way a prince might be if princes ever managed to live unashamedly among fountains and marbled halls, so adored that they returned adoration automatically, as a matter of course, because they had known nothing else.

Less than an hour later the little extended family prepared to leave. We watched, surreptitiously, as Uncle Donald woke the child, set him on his feet again, stroked his hair. We watched then as Donald put on baggy chinos and a polo shirt, as he plopped a dramatically unflattering canvas hat on his head. Standing, in clothes, he slouched. They departed, with the child scampering and cavorting around the object of his affections, who had by then transformed himself into a citizen in poly-blends; a regular guy, unenchanted, with ordinary features (we saw, once he was dressed, that he in fact had a pleasant but unremarkable face, with too much chin for its modest nose and too much forehead for its close-set eyes); someone you wouldn't glance at twice on the street. He went off (I imagine) to join the multitude of others cruising the streets or nursing beers in the semidark at the edges of dance floors; off to hope and wish and wonder; to admire the flashier guys dancing shirtless or laughing heedlessly with their packs of friends; to try his luck along with everybody else who was out there, the whole wistful, unruly crew, looking for love in all the wrong places.

THE BEECH FOREST

If you go straight on the dune trail and skip Race Point, you will eventually reach the beech forest. There is a clear point of demarcation between the sand and the woods it has partially engulfed. First you will see what appear to be outcroppings of bare twigs protruding from the sand— these are the tops of dead trees. Several yards farther on you will see dead trees mired to their lower branches in sand, and then trees that are covered only halfway up their trunks, still alive but beginning to die. Then you will be among the living trees. The sand-glacier in the beech forest has been more or less halted by conservationists, but the dunes north of the forest remain in motion. On old maps you can locate buried forests, and walk across pristine dunes with deceased forests inside them.

The beech forest in summer is shady and slightly dank; it is full of a greened, deepened light. The smell changes from dusty pine to a fermented odor of pine tar, decomposing leaves, and an indefinable, organic rankness that resembles, at its most potent, the smell of a wet dog. You will pass a shallow pond that freezes over in winter and that wears, in summer, a skin of pale green lily pads with trumpet-shaped flowers—yellow at the edges of the pond, white in the slightly deeper water toward the middle. You can stay on the narrow asphalt bike trail, or you can leave your bike and wander into the woods along any of the sandy paths that meander off among the trees. If you do that, you'll quickly find yourself walking among tupelo and inkberry, white oaks and red maples, as well as the eponymous beech trees, all of which form surprisingly orderly hallways and small, roomlike clearings, with lush carpets of fallen leaves and canopies of branches thick enough to shelter you in a rainstorm. It would not be entirely surprising to find chairs and lamps out there, and a table set for tea. People sometimes get married in these clearings, and local children go there for all the childish purposes that require concealment. The trunks of the trees are covered with carvings: initials and obscenities; various assertions that so-and-so was here, in 1990 or 1975 or 1969; declarations of eternal love to vanished objects named Jim, Carol, Drew, Calla, Tom, Ken, and Lindy, among others. The old ones, from the fifties and sixties, have all but faded into the bark—they look like name-shaped scars manifested by the trees themselves. The newer ones are various shades of gray, depending on their age. Only the very recent names are raw and white, though they too, of course, will fade.

SNAIL ROAD

The last wild place on land I want to tell you about is the dune at the end of Snail Road. Snail Road is actually a dirt path, though wide enough to accommodate a car, and you can in fact park your car there if you need to. It is on the East End of town, on the far side of the highway. The path is arcaded by the branches of trees. At its far end stands the dune known as Mt. Ararat, a single, titanic rise of sand, utterly barren. It could be a dune in the Sahara.

This is another of those strangely potent places. Everyone I know who has spent any time on the dune agrees that there's, well, *something* there, though outwardly it is neither more nor less than an enormous arc of sand cutting across the sky. Climb to the top of it. On one side you'll see the treetops and rooftops of town; on the other you'll look across a span of lesser dunes to the Atlantic. To the east, in the direction of Truro, is Pilgrim Lake, though you can't quite see it from atop Mt. Ararat. Pilgrim Lake was once East Harbor but is now, essentially, an enormous puddle. About 150 years ago, the town fathers realized that windblown sand was accumulating in East Harbor in such quantities that it threatened not only to render the harbor too shallow for boats but might extend out along the coast and spoil all of Provincetown's harbor. So they diked off East Harbor and laid railroad tracks on the new embankment that separated it from the open water. The only road into Provincetown still runs along that embankment, parallel to the long-vanished train tracks.

Being stilled and sourceless, Pilgrim Lake feels vaguely sinister. It is Provincetown's Dead Sea. Although it is every bit as bright in sunlight as the ocean from which it has been separated, it shimmers differently. It is steelier, more opaque. From the dune at the end of Snail Road, you are surrounded by the Atlantic in three different aspects: the ocean proper, the bay, and the brackish lake.

The lunar stillness that pervades out there is difficult to describe. It involves a repose that is pleasurable without being exactly comforting. You feel as if you are in the eye of something. You are aware—I am aware, anyway—of the world as a place that doesn't know or care that it's beautiful, that produces beauty incidentally while pursuing its true imperatives to simply exist and change; a world that is, more than anything else, silent and unpopulated as it lives according to geological time. You feel, momentarily, what I imagine nomads might feel as they cross the desert. You are at home, and you are at the same time in a place too full of its own eternal business, too old and too young, to notice whether you live or die, you with your pots and pans and rugs and bells.

The Snakes of September

All summer I heard them
rustling in the shrubbery,
outracing me from tier
to tier in my garden,
a whisper among the viburnums,
a signal flashed from the hedgerow,
a shadow pulsing
in the barberry thicket.
Now that the nights are chill
and the annuals spent,
I should have thought them gone,
in a torpor of blood
slipped to the nether world
before the sickle frost.
Not so. In the deceptive balm
of noon, as if defiant of the curse
that spoiled another garden,
these two appear on show
through a narrow slit
in the dense green brocade
of a north-country spruce,

dangling head-down, entwined
in a brazen love-knot.
I put out my hand and stroke
the fine, dry grit of their skins.
After all,
we are partners in this land,
co-signers of a covenant.
At my touch the wild
braid of creation
trembles.

STANLEY KUNITZ

The Town

PROVINCETOWN IS, HAS always been, an eccentrics' sanctuary, more or less the way other places are bird sanctuaries or wild game preserves. It is the only small town I know of where those who live unconventionally seem to outnumber those who live within the prescribed boundaries of home and licensed marriage, respectable job and biological children. It is where people who were the outcasts and untouchables in other towns can become prominent members of society. Until recently it was possible to live there cheaply and well, and it has long been possible for, say, two men to walk down Commercial Street holding hands and carrying their adopted Peruvian baby without exciting any unusual degree of interest.

It has been attracting refugees, rebels, and visionaries for almost four hundred years.

THE PILGRIM MOTHERS AND FATHERS

Provincetown's first settlers were, in fact, the Pilgrims, who sailed the *Mayflower* into Provincetown Harbor in 1620. They spent the winter there but, finding too little fresh water, sailed that spring to Plymouth, which has gone into the history books as the Pilgrims' initial point of disembarkation. Provincetown is, understandably, not happy about this misrepresentation of the facts.

The *Mayflower* arrived in what is now Provincetown Harbor after sixty-six days at sea. The Pilgrims' reaction seems to have been less than rapturous. One of them wrote that the landscape was full of "shrubbie pines, hurts [huckleberries], and such trash." That winter, the Mayflower Compact was drawn up. A baby, Peregrine White, was born, and four people—Dorothy Bradford, James Chilton, Jasper Moore, and Edward Thompson—died. The latter three are buried in Provincetown. Dorothy Bradford went overboard and is believed to have committed suicide.

The *Mayflower* was a cargo ship, not meant for passengers, and so was available for relatively little money. The people we now know as the Pilgrims had first left England for Holland in search of religious freedom but had spent twelve years failing to find work there before deciding, in desperation, to sail to the New World. They were not Puritans; they called themselves "separatists," and while they were a relatively serious group, they were not as stern as Puritans. They danced and played games. They were not averse to a little color in their dress.

Only about a third of them were separatists. The other two-thirds were people the separatists referred to as "strangers," men and women who for one reason or another had failed to prosper in England and so came along on the *Mayflower* hoping to do better for themselves. The Pilgrims needed them to help pay for the boat. The majority of the Founding Fathers and Mothers were, from the very beginning, looking to make a buck. Less than a decade after its founding, the settlement at Plymouth was rife with robbery, alcoholism, and sex in all its unsanctioned forms. In his *History of Plymouth Plantation,* William Bradford, Dorothy's widower, complained about "incontinency between persons unmarried . . . but some married persons also. But that which is worse, even sodomy and buggery (things fearful to name) have broke forth in this land oftener than once."

Provincetown has gone as unmentioned in this particular chapter of the American story as have the habits and proclivities of the Founding Fathers. Every Thanksgiving innumerable American schoolchildren produce paintings, dioramas, and pageants about the Pilgrims' landing at Plymouth Rock, but it would be the rare child who has ever heard the name Provincetown. At the beginning of the twentieth century, the town fathers tried to rectify the situation by building an enormous monument to the Pilgrims.

They held a national design competition, but all the submissions were variations on an obelisk, which was considered too much like the Washington Monument. The selectmen decided, for reasons that have not survived, on a replica of the Torre del Mangla in Siena, which stands in the Tuscan square where Dante once walked and where the *palio,* the chaotic annual horse race, is held. President Teddy Roosevelt laid the cornerstone in 1907, amid much fanfare; the tower was finished in 1910. It has become Provincetown's identifying symbol, the anchor of the town, though it has not had the desired effect of educating the general public about the *Mayflower's* first point of disembarkation on this continent. Few people have made the connection between an Italian bell tower and the Pilgrims' landing.

The Pilgrim Monument is visible almost everywhere, in town and in the wild. If you look at it from the proper angle—obliquely, from any of its four corners—you can see the head of Donald Duck. The top of the tower is his hat, the arches are his eyes, and the crenelations under the arches are his beak. The Donald Duck head is slightly difficult to see, but once you've seen it, you can't look at the Monument and see anything else.

THE LIVING

Provincetown has been rambunctious, remote, and amenable to outsiders for as long as it has existed. It was originally part of Truro, the next town over, but in 1727 Truro disgustedly drew a line at Beach Point, and the resulting sliver of loose morals and questionable practices was called Provincetown, over the protests of its citizens, who preferred the name Herringtown. Being inexpensive and loose, it has long attracted artists, who continue to compose a larger percentage of the general population than any other city or town I can think of. Eugene O'Neill lived there when he was a young, unknown alcoholic struggling to write plays; Tennessee Williams summered there when he was a world-famous alcoholic struggling to write plays. Milton Avery, Charles Hawthorne, Hans Hofmann, Robert Motherwell, and Mark Rothko have lived there, as have Edmund Wilson, John Reed, John Waters, Denis Johnson, and Divine. Norman Mailer, Stanley Kunitz, Mary Oliver, and Mark Doty live there still.

Among the less well known are Radio Girl, who walked the streets announcing the news she received from a radio in her head, and a woman who then called herself Sick, who lived in a treehouse she and her friends built in a big tree off Bradford Street and who kept her name but altered the spelling and pronunciation, to Sique (pronounced Seek) when she met and married the head of the art department at a big university and suddenly found herself transported from a life as a neo-hippie wild woman to one that involved giving parties for academics in southern California. Still today the Inside-Out Man, a citizen of sixty or so with a full beard and a tendency to dress for winter no matter what the season, walks along the East End of town, sweeping the sidewalks with furious concentration, wearing all his clothes inside out.

In summer the streets of Provincetown are as crowded as a carnival midway, and the people who make up the crowds are largely Caucasian. This is Cape Cod, a kingdom of white people, and that is among its more problematic aspects. This strangeness has been heightened, recently, by the practice of bringing in Jamaican workers for the summers, mostly to do the low-paying kitchen work no one else is willing to do. Some of the Jamaicans who come to work in Provincetown for the summer have taken up year-round residence, and it seems possible—it does not seem impossible—that the following reversal is gradually taking place: the white gay men and lesbians, who for so long were the itinerants and outsiders, tend now to own most of the businesses and much of the real estate in town, and the Jamaican immigrants are establishing themselves as the new, marginalized, defiantly embedded population.

Among the strollers and shoppers on a summer afternoon, it is not unusual to see, within a fifty-foot radius, all of the following: a crowd of elderly tourists who have come for the day on a tour bus or have disembarked from a cruise ship anchored in the harbor; a pack of muscle boys on their way to the gym; a vacationing mother and father shepherding their exhausted and fussy children through the shops; a pair of lesbians with a dachshund in a rainbow collar; two gay dads in chinos and Izod shirts pushing their adopted daughter in a stroller; a dreadlocked and ostentatiously tattooed young woman who works at the head shop; a man dressed, very convincingly, as Celine Dion; elderly women doing errands; several closeted schoolteachers from various parts of the country who come to Provincetown for two weeks every year to escape the need for secrecy; several weary fishermen coming home from their stints on a scallop boat; a bond trader in three-hundred-dollar sandals, up for the weekend from New York; and a brigade of furious local kids on skateboards, seeing how close they can come to the pedestrians without actually knocking one over, a stunt that is usually but not always successful.

After Labor Day the crowds diminish considerably, except for holiday weekends, and the town is gradually given over again to its year-round residents. For those who've decided to settle there, Provincetown is an impoverished mother, gentle and loving; an old ribald mother who's been through too much to be shocked by any habits you've acquired in the larger world and who will share with you whatever she's got, though she lives on little herself and can't keep much food in the house these days. Year-round jobs are scarce, and the ones that do exist tend to numb the brain. Most people work two or three jobs in the summers. If you work for wages in Provincetown, it's not unusual to find yourself cleaning a guest house in the mornings, taking an hour off, and then going to your waiter job until midnight. You get through the winters on savings and unemployment checks.

Uncountable numbers of young or no-longer-young people have gone there to escape situations they could no longer tolerate—addictions or dead-end jobs or discouraging love affairs, whatever questionable fate they seemed to have made for themselves—or simply to take a break from their tolerably difficult lives and dwell for a while in peace. People often move there after their patience, their energy, or their greed have been exhausted elsewhere. The woman who makes stained-glass Christmas ornaments and sells them at crafts fairs may once have been a corporate attorney; the man laboring over his poetry and working nights in a restaurant may once have been an advertising executive. Provincetown's hierarchies of class and status are more liquid than they are in most places. The girl who cleared your table at the restaurant where you had breakfast is seated next to you at the dinner party you go to that night.

Although it is as difficult to live anonymously within the borders of Provincetown as it is in any small town, it is one of the places in the world you can disappear into. It is the Morocco of America, the New Orleans of the north. While the people of Provincetown are capable of holding grudges with Olympian fervor—your sins may be forgiven there, but they are rarely forgotten—it is ruled fundamentally by kindness and a respect for idiosyncrasy. Bad behavior is frowned upon; unorthodoxy is not. A male-to-female transsexual may stand in line at the A&P behind a woman trying to manage her three unruly children, and no one thinks anything of it. They are both buying the same brands of cat food and yogurt.

You are safe in Provincetown, in just about every sense of the word. In the literal sense it is almost entirely free of crime (with the notable exception of a thriving bicycle-stealing industry—if you leave your bike unlocked overnight, you have more or less already sent it to any one of a number of unknowable used-bicycle shops up Cape). In a subtler way, at least in part because Provincetown has not thrived since its whales were slaughtered, the town at large attaches no outstanding sense of shame to those who break down or give up; who cannot cope or don't care to cope; who decide it would be easier or simply more fun to stop going out in daylight or to grow a chest-length beard and wear dresses or to sing in public whenever they feel a song coming on.

Most people who come looking for respite stay a year or two or three and move on, because they've gotten what they came for or because they can't take the winter silence or can't find a decent job or because they've found that they brought with them the very things they'd meant to escape. Some, however, have settled in. Some of the elderly sitting on the benches in front of Town Hall were once young criminals or outpatients who thought they were coming to Provincetown to regather their energies in a cheap apartment with a water view, maybe try writing some poetry or music, catch their breath, and then move on.

Apart from the descendants of Portuguese fishermen, who have been there for generations but keep very much to themselves, almost everyone in Provincetown is a transplant. I have rarely met anyone who was born there, though I know many who consider it their true home and who treat their earlier lives either as extended mistakes finally made right by moving to Provincetown or as prolonged periods of incubation during which their genetic strands were gradually stitched into the fabric of character needed for them to be born as themselves, fully formed, right here. Provincetown is, in this regard, an anomaly—it is a village every bit as distinct and habit-bound as villages in Sicily or County Kerry but one that routinely accepts newcomers and grants them unequivocal rights of citizenship.

Among its transplanted residents Provincetown tends to inspire the sort of patriotism associated with small struggling nations. Those who live there usually defend it ferociously to outsiders and complain about it only among themselves. It is cantankerously devoted to its quirks and traditions, and like many places in love with their own ways of doing and being, it has predicted its own downfall almost from the day it was founded. In the mid-1800s, when a wooden sidewalk was built along one side of the sand road that eventually became Commercial Street, it aroused such dismay over what it portended about the loss of Provincetown's soul that a number of citizens refused to walk on it and trudged resolutely through the ankle-deep sand all their lives. In the twenty-plus years I've been going there, I have heard the town's imminent demise predicted over and over again. It is dying because its waters are fished out. It is dying because it has no jobs. It is dying because artists no longer live there in sufficient numbers. It is dying because it is beginning to prosper but at the hands of the wrong sort of people—rich people who live in cities and want to use Provincetown only as a summer refuge. It is dying because its soul is exhausted, because its schools are no good, because so many have been taken by the AIDS epidemic, because no one can afford the rents.

Some members of the P-town population (it is, by the way, perfectly all right to call it "P-town") live according to a central simplicity as absolute as creed. They prefer earnestness to irony, the local to the immense. Provincetown lives at a bemused distance from the rest of the country. It does not quite consider itself American, and in this regard it is probably more right than wrong. Last summer I found a pair of quotation marks at the flea market in Wellfleet. They had come from a movie marquee. They were eight inches high, glossy black; they had a bulky, elderly symmetry. I gave them to Melanie, believing she'd know what to do with them. She was on her way to California then, and she took one pair of quotation marks with her, to leave behind in San Francisco. She keeps the other pair in Provincetown.

☆

ALTHOUGH IT'S BETTER known for its gayness than for its heterosexuality, Provincetown is home to a considerable quotient of straight people, and everyone lives pretty much in peace. Just as the Log Cabin Republican not only can't ignore the existence of stone butches but buys his coffee from one every morning, straight people and gay people are all passengers on the same ship and couldn't remain separate even if they'd like to. At its best

Provincetown can feel like an improved version of the world at large, a version in which sexuality, though always important, is not much of a deciding factor. For several years, long ago, I played poker every Wednesday night at the home of Chris Magriel, a woman in her seventies who lived in a den of paisley shawls, embroidered pillows, and elderly stuffed animals. I was coming out then, unable to broach the subject with my family, and when I told Chris I thought I was gay, her milky blue eyes deepened in thought and she said, "Well, dear, if I was your age, I'd want to try it, too." She didn't embrace or console me. She simply treated it as the matter of small concern I'd hoped it might be. I told her about the man I was dating. She said, "He sounds very nice." Then we started laying out food for the other poker players, who were due to arrive at any moment.

In summer the straight tourists are generally as amused by the more flamboyant members of the population as they are meant to be. It's common to see someone taking a picture of his mother, a champagne blonde in jeans and Reeboks, with her arm cheerfully around the shoulders of a man dressed as Cher. Last summer in the West End I passed a drag queen who was flyering for a show (*flyering* is a nonverb you hear frequently in Provincetown—it refers to the act of distributing flyers that advertise a show, often involving costumes to excite interest in same). The man in question, an extremely tall man wearing Minnie Mouse eyelashes and a blue beehive wig that made him just under eight feet high, stood before a raptly attentive

boy about four years old. "All right," the man in the
wig said, "but this is the last time I'm doing it." He lifted
his wig off his head and showed the child the crew cut
underneath. The child fell into paroxysms of laughter.
The man replaced his wig and walked on.

☆

PROVINCETOWN'S LARGE, DISORDERLY party of
transients, émigrés, tourists, summer homeowners, et
cetera goes on at an almost total remove, in every sense
but the geographical, from the generally more settled lives
of the people who were born there and who are mostly
the descendants of Portuguese immigrants from the
Azores. When the whaling industry was annihilated by
the rise of petroleum oil in the mid-1800s, Provincetown
became a fishing village, and the population came to be
dominated by the Portuguese whose families had fished
for centuries. They thrived there until recently, when the
waters around Provincetown were almost entirely fished
out; now many of the Portuguese American citizens live
in several small enclaves on the far side of Bradford Street.
The more prosperous among them run most of the oper-
ations that require year-round residence. They operate the
gas and oil companies and own or staff the banks and
markets and drugstores. When, in her 1942 book *Time
and the Town,* the only book I know about Provincetown,
Mary Heaton Vorse referred to them as "Dark faces on
the streets, beautiful dark-eyed girls who love color and

who make the streets gay with their bright dresses and
their laughter," I suspect she meant it as a compliment.
These "colorful characters" are now the old guard, the
town's most respectable and conservative citizens. The same
names, some of them Anglicized more than two hundred
years ago, appear over and over again on the tombstones
in the town cemetery: Atkins, Avellar, Cabral, Cook,
Days, Enos, Rose, Tasha, Silva, Snow.

From Nowhere

I think the sea is a useless teacher, pitching and falling
no matter the weather, when our lives are rather lakes

unlocking in a constant and bewildering spring. Listen,
a day comes, when you say what all winter

I've been meaning to ask, and a crack booms and echoes
where ice had seemed solid, scattering ducks

and scaring us half to death. In Vermont, you dreamed
from the crown of a hill and across a ravine

you saw lights so familiar they might have been ours
shining back from the future.

And waking, you walked there, to the real place,
and when you saw only trees, came back bleak

with a foreknowledge we have both come to believe in.
But this morning, a kind day has descended, from nowhere,

and making coffee in the usual way, measuring grounds
with the wooden spoon, I remembered,

this is how things happen, cup by cup, familiar gesture
after gesture, what else can we know of safety

or of fruitfulness? We walk with mincing steps within
a thaw as slow as February, wading through currents

that surprise us with their sudden warmth. Remember,
last week you woke still whistling for a bird

that had miraculously escaped its cage, and look, today,
a swallow has come to settle behind this rented rain gutter,

gripping a twig twice his size in his beak, staggering
under its weight, so delicately, so precariously, it seems

from here, holding all he knows in his mouth.

MARIE HOWE

Animals

*I*N ADDITION TO its human population, Provincetown is home to a number of thriving animal contin-
gents. It is a big dog town, the sort of place where local
dogs (a standard poodle named Dorothy, a black Labrador
mix known as Lucy, the long-haired dachshund of the
portly man who walks the streets in caftans) are as thoroughly known in their idiosyncrasies of being as the residents and are just as likely to be greeted by name if they
saunter into a shop or café.

Provincetown also boasts a considerable cohort of
stately cats, more often than not white with bold black
markings, like living Franz Kline paintings, descendants
of a long-gone ur-cat. The cats possess, in toto, whatever
remains of the placid, burgherish entitlement of the old
whaling captains. Dogs, though abundant in Provincetown, do not rule, at least in part because strictly enforced
leash laws, which apply even on the beaches, keep them
forever relegated to the status of pet. They are named and

numbered—they are always at least slightly humiliated. The cats, being freer and more ubiquitous, are not visibly owned at all, and they travel the streets and beaches with aristocratic certainty. They are beauties, these cats. There is, in Provincetown, almost no visible evidence of the scrawnier, more ferretlike and skittish specimens—I can only imagine that those nervous, bony types are relegated to alleys and backyards by their more prosperous brothers and sisters, the great glossy fifteen-pounders with royal heads and heavy, voluptuous tails who are never spooked by dogs or pedestrians; who are prone, on occasion, to nap in the middle of a sun-warmed street.

As for wild animals, Provincetown is most prominently host to a thriving population of skunks. Skunks are everywhere there. Since they are nocturnal, you won't ever encounter a skunk in daylight, but if you walk around late at night, after eleven or so, when the streets have begun to empty, you can hardly avoid seeing one or two or more. Though they fully possess their own animal dignity and sport those white stripes that go incandescent in the streetlight, they are not the most imposing of creatures. They are among nature's pedestrians and trash-pickers. They waddle brazenly back and forth across Commercial Street, right in the middle of town, scavenging. If you leave them alone and go about your business, they will do the same.

The residents dogs know better, but visiting dogs, being uninformed about the consequences, often chase skunks, and of course, just when they've got one cornered, as they are congratulating themselves on their courage and skill, the worst happens. One summer Kenny and I were having dinner with friends when our host's Scottie was sprayed by a skunk. Since the dog's owner was too drunk and stoned at the time to do much beyond register his dismay, Kenny and I took care of it as best we could. We had heard tomato juice was the only remedy, and so we rounded up all the tomato juice we could get from the neighbors, though we had to fall back on ketchup, tomato puree, and tomato soup, since actual tomato juice was not available in the required amounts. We put the dog in a tin basin and poured all the tomato products over her. It worked, more or less, but I can tell you that a skunk's spray, close up, has a quality entirely different from those zones of reek you may have passed through on highways. It is worse than foul. It is the smell of annihilation. It has no parallel I can think of. It isn't rot, it isn't sulphur or ammonia; it is just indescribably bad, in a category of its own. You taste it when you breathe. You feel it infiltrating your nose and lungs. It was, in its way, a remarkable experience, though I wouldn't care to repeat it. It was a reminder, the most potent one imaginable, that nature is very good at what it does; that that which survives is so clearly meant to do so.

If skunks and cats are the petite bourgeoisie of Provincetown, its most stolid and crankily respectable non-human citizens, other animals live there at a more ephemeral but insistent remove. On the remoter edges you may see a fox every now and then, bright russet, usually standing so still (it will have heard you coming as if you were a freight train) that you may not be sure, at first, that it's a living thing at all—it is the very embodiment of the word *attention*. I have seen deer out in the dunes and, once, a doe and fawn browsing among the grass in the cemetery.

A hardy population of racoons and opossums and the occasional coyote moves more furtively than the skunks but with similar determination among the scraps and leftovers of late-night Provincetown. Late one night last summer, when my friend James and I had gone to retrieve our bicycles from where we'd left them, on the lawn in front of the Universalist church, an opossum came out of the bushes and stood directly in front of me. It was young, not by any means a baby but far from fully grown; it was an adolescent. It stood less than two feet before me, looking at me with an expression neither friendly nor fearful. It seemed merely curious. It was pale gray, almost white, with a shovel-shaped head, a nose the color of a pencil eraser, and eyes that were perfect black beads. We made eye contact. This has never happened to me with a wild animal. Automatically, without thinking, I reached over and touched it, gently, on the top of its head. I wasn't petting it. I was trying to acknowledge it, to be polite, the way you might try to communicate not just your friendliness but your beingness to an extraterrestrial. It was foolish; I did it without thinking. The opossum's pelt was rough but not unpleasantly so, like the bristles of a paintbrush. It didn't bite me, but it did not like being touched; touching it had clearly not been the correct gesture. Still, it did not bolt away in terror. It simply slipped back into the bushes, and I went on to catch up with James.

The West End

ALTHOUGH IT IS now a semiorderly concentration of shops and houses, Provincetown was once so thoroughly devoted to the sea and what it yields as to seem as much a manifestation of the water as a human settlement. During its first hundred years, until the early 1800s, it was not really divided up into streets per se; it was simply a gathering of houses and shops, built on whatever patch of sand their builders selected. Gutted cod for salt cod, one of Provincetown's most profitable early exports, lay drying on the sand before most of the houses, and cod hung drying from the trees as well. By way of ornamentation, most of the houses offered whale ribs and vertebrae in the stretches of sand where their gardens would have been.

Soil came to Provincetown by way of ships that sailed there from Europe and South America, to load up on salt cod. They carried earth in their holds for ballast, which local citizens were glad to purchase, to spread around their houses for gardens. The ships' crews refilled their holds with rocks for their return trips. This practice was outlawed as Provincetown became so denuded of rocks that the tides began to encroach upon the houses, but by then the selling of dirt had become a profitable sideline among the crews of the foreign ships. They continued selling earth to the people of Provincetown and stole rocks from the beaches at night.

Provincetown has always divided itself into West End and East End. On this walk start at the West End and work your way east. The West End was traditionally, literally, the wrong side of the tracks. When Provincetown had become a significant whaling port, in the mid- and late 1800s, the most prosperous town in the state of Massachusetts, railroad tracks ran along the Cape right out onto MacMillan Wharf, in the middle of town, so trains could load whale oil, bone, and baleen directly into boxcars. (The trains are by now long gone.) The whaling crews and fishermen, the laborers and clerks and servants, many of them Portuguese, all lived west of the railroad tracks. The wealthy—the whaling captains and merchants, the summer people from Boston and New York—all lived to the east. Most of the gentry never went west of the tracks. It was considered dangerous, and an upstanding member of society seen venturing in that direction could only be after something unseemly.

A version of the old division—reputable versus disreputable—remains, though it no longer has as much to do with economics. Compared to the East End, the West

End is younger, sexier, and a bit more prone to noise at night though not, by any urban standards, very noisy at all. It is more gay. The beach where men go to have sex after the bars close is on the West End.

The West End, though every bit as densely inhabited as the East End, is slightly rougher and more random. The houses are more various, since the neighborhood's history is not as genteel or orderly. You could say that the West End is more American, for better and for worse; it is a bit like West Egg in *The Great Gatsby,* where Jay Gatsby lived; where the newly rich and the newly arrived squeeze their private, personal monuments in among the prim cottages that came over from Long Point 150 years ago. The East End, like East Egg, where Daisy Buchanan lived, is more Cape Cod, more in love with tradition, more likely to house people whose families have owned their shingled, dormered residences for fifty or a hundred years.

JOHN'S HOUSE

On the West End of Commercial Street is my favorite Provincetown house, the home of my friend John Dowd. John's house stands at the bend in Commercial Street that resulted when, in the mid-1800s, a particularly stubborn citizen refused to move his salt works to accommodate the laying out of the street (which was then called Front Street, as Bradford was sensibly called Back Street).

John is a landscape painter. When he bought his house ten years ago, it was one of the eyesores of town, though the term *eyesore* probably implies a grander awfulness than this house actually possessed. It was simply as devoid of character or charm as a house can be: an old rambling building wrapped in aluminum siding, with a faded asphalt roof. If it were a person, it would have been a server in a high school cafeteria or an attendant at the sort of nursing home you hope never to have to go to; someone stolid and blank, of questionable competence, whose uniform is not quite clean and whose manner suggests a state of exhausted boredom so extreme that an emotion as deep as despair would be a relief.

No one I know thought it was a good idea for John to buy this place, even though the price was low (as, we all felt, it well should have been). Everyone I know is astonished at the house John was able to find under all that aluminum and asphalt, that general air of quiet hopelessness. It turns out that aluminum siding peels off, as John put it, "like foil off a baked potato," and in this case had actually helped preserve the old wood siding beneath. He replaced the aluminum-frame windows, the sort you find in cheap condos, with six-over-sixes he scavenged from flea markets and demolitions and managed to fill with panes of the imperfect, slightly wavy glass they would have held when they were new. He put up shutters (also old scavenged ones, from the period when the house was built), replaced the roof, and added a back porch.

As a renovator, John's true gift lies in his respect for the process of decay. Provincetown is full of "restored" houses that, with every good intention on the part of their owners, have been rendered so pristine, they might be part of a Cape Cod village section in Epcot Center. John's aesthetic runs more toward the Miss Havisham, and his house is not only lovely but looks as if it has been standing there, more or less unaltered, for at least a hundred years.

Usually in summer someone is staying there, in one of the upstairs bedrooms with an old brass bed and a dormer window. Often more than one or two people are staying there. It is a bit like I imagine English country houses to have been during the days of Jane Austen—a sort of ongoing semiparty with guests who come and go, read books in the garden or cook some dish they're renowned for, gather at dinnertime, and then disperse again. One guest, an erudite man and a considerable cook, somehow extended his visit to just under four years.

The house has a well-used music room with a player piano and a big closet devoted entirely to costumes. It is possible, at John's house, to arrive in your street clothes and emerge as a sultan, a Confederate soldier, or a ballerina with feathered wings. The archway that leads from his reading room to the living room has been fitted out with heavy velvet curtains that facilitate the occasional parlor game, play, or evening of tableaux vivants.

If you happen to be in Provincetown on the Fourth of July, you will find a group of us installed on John's front porch, under the enormous, tattered American flag he hangs every July over his front door, with only forty-five stars on it. It is one of our traditions. We have a grill and a good supply of hot dogs—anyone who wants one is welcome to a hot dog and a glass of whatever we're serving, if you eat such things and care to linger awhile. We play instruments, very badly, and only until the irritable man three doors down calls the police and makes us stop, though if you arrive before the police do, we'd love for you to take a turn on the drum, saxophone, tambourine, or kazoo. It doesn't matter if you can't play. None of us can.

In one of the upstairs windows, the one that looks right up Commercial Street, John has placed a chalky old marble bust of Shakespeare, looking out. You can see it especially well late at night, when everyone has finally gone to bed and Shakespeare shines palely in the dark window, like a little moon.

Downtown

*I*F YOU START on the West End and walk east on Commercial Street, you'll find that shops and galleries begin to appear among the houses. By the time you reach the intersection of Commercial and Winslow streets, you are in the full-blown commercial district. If you are there during the tourist season, you will find yourself among thicker and thicker crowds until, by the time you reach Town Hall, it will be impossible to walk in any reasonably efficient straight line for more than three or four paces.

For decades there has been an ongoing battle waged by some citizens to have Commercial Street closed to vehicular traffic, but as far as I can see, that will never happen. Commercial is a one-way street—traffic moves from east to west—that has not been widened since it was laid out 150 years ago, well before the birth of the Jeep Cherokee. There is a sidewalk on only one side, and it barely accommodates two average-sized adults walking side by side. Commercial Street faces a considerable challenge as a main thoroughfare for multitudes of strolling pedestrians, families with strollers, bicyclists, delivery trucks, and needlessly large American cars.

The crowds on Commercial Street are extremely difficult to negotiate if you're trying to arrive at any sort of actual destination with anything resembling alacrity. The people walking along the street are, naturally, almost all browsers and sightseers. They make frequent unscheduled stops. They don't understand that Commercial Street is, in fact, a street (who can blame them?), and so they wander from side to side—riding through on a bicycle (the preferred and most practical mode of transportation in Provincetown) is like flying a spaceship through a field of sluggish but erratically moving asteroids.

Although the town welcomes these people, needs them for its very livelihood, residents tend to become irritable about the crowds, especially as summer wears on, when the street on which they conduct their necessary business is all but impassable, and the purchase of any rudimentary grocery item may involve waiting in line for half an hour or longer. A visitor strolling on Commercial Street on a summer day should not feel unduly offended if a citizen scowls or mutters as he or she attempts to negotiate the street in order to buy a newspaper or a carton of milk or go to the post office. It isn't personal; not exactly personal. As a tourist, you are part of the stormy weather that blows through every year, and residents feel as free as anyone anywhere to complain about the weather, knowing, as everyone does everywhere, that their feelings won't make one bit of difference to the elements at large.

A Blessing from the Post Office

The Provincetown post office is in the western half of town. For many years one of the women who worked there (I'm sorry to say she has retired) wrote poetry and loved anyone else who wrote poetry, whether they were any good at it or not. If you were sending your poems out in hopes of publication or a grant, and you told her that that was what you were doing, she'd take your envelope into the back of the post office and press it to her bare breast for luck before sending it on.

Places to Pee

There are, as far as I know, only two places where the public is officially permitted to pee without buying anything. You can use the bathrooms in Town Hall, though it closes to the public if a meeting, show, or fund-raising auction is going on inside. There are, more reliably, public bathrooms on the bay side of Town Hall, right by the parking lot next to MacMillan Wharf.

Gossip

Provincetown is, among its many attributes, one of the more impressive rumor mills in the Western world. Nathaniel Parker Willis, a popular nineteenth-century journalist, said over a hundred years ago that it was a place with "no secrets, where there is but one accountable path in the whole neighborhood. Everybody at Provincetown knows every time everybody goes out, and every time anybody comes in." That is still true. Any small town engenders a good deal of gossip, but in this regard Provincetown is to other towns what McDonald's is to mom-and-pop diners. Most citizens of most small towns must content themselves with a handful of extramarital affairs and a few wayward sons and daughters; they must chew and chew this limited fare. In Provincetown the denizens tend to lead more dramatic lives, and some citizens maintain a more than usually creative relationship to reality. Thus, the offerings are almost embarrassingly rich and varied.

The nerve center of Provincetown's gossip network is the steps in front of the post office. They were, however, better suited to leisurely tale-telling before post office officials, in an act I can only interpret as conspicuous malice, became concerned that loiterers were interfering with the public's ability to come and go and so cut the steps in half by installing a wholly unnecessary brick flower box. In response, satellite gossip stations have been established—the bricked yard in front of Joe's coffee house (the one in the West End, not its sister to the east) and the wooden bench in front of a store called Map are especially fertile.

The gossip season extends from early fall to late spring. In summer, during the tourist assault, everyone is too busy to pay more than glancing attention to questions about who's doing what to whom and why. By mid-September, however, the feast begins, and it goes on well into June. In a month of average fecundity, someone will have left a lover for that person's former lover, someone will have gotten drunk and trashed the apartment of an ex, someone will have gotten fired under suspicious circumstances rumored to involve sex or drugs or both, and the members of a newly formed theatrical troupe will have had a screaming fight, disbanded, and then re-formed minus the member considered to be the source of the trouble. The meetings of various twelve-step programs around town have a problem with people who are not really addicts at all but say they are so they can come to meetings and find out what's going on. During the time it took me to write this chapter on gossip, I received a number of e-mails from several friends in Provincetown who feel particularly obliged to keep me informed. One concerned a young man who stole a car on Commercial Street, crashed it into a van carrying deaf tourists, and ran out into the bay, believing that would throw dogs off his scent. The second involved two local men who took a taxi to one of the banks, put on ski masks, and held up the tellers at gunpoint. The men forced the tellers to fill several garbage bags with currency, then got on two getaway bicycles they had left nearby, rode home with the loot, where they were quickly apprehended. Both those stories are true. I checked.

Among the more notable rumors I've heard over the years, I offer the following:

Barbra Streisand is buying a house, under an assumed name, in North Truro.

Elton John is trying to buy a house in Provincetown but can't find one he likes.

Provincetown is one of the designated areas for the federal Witness Protection Program, and many of its innocous-seeming citizens (to whatever extent anyone in Provincetown can be called innocuous) have informed on members of crime syndicates and been resettled in Provincetown with new identities.

Jackie Onassis once showed up at the A-House with Gore Vidal and a phalanx of bodyguards.

It should also be noted that there is always a celebrity who has been seen with absolute certainty somewhere in town. These sightings have ranged, over the years, from Kevin Spacey to Madonna, Elizabeth Taylor, Goldie Hawn (with and without Kurt Russell), and, perennially, Barbra Streisand. The only celebrity I have ever seen there is Gene Rayburn, former host of *The Match Game,* gliding down Commercial Street on Rollerblades.

Conversation in general, which includes but is not limited to gossip, is both valued and widely practiced in Provincetown. Its citizens are a loquacious people, fond of stories of all kinds. It is common for a Provincetownian driving along Commercial Street to see a friend passing on foot or on a bicycle and stop to talk to that person at medium length. If you are in a car behind one of these impromptu klatsches, please do not honk your horn, unless the conversation goes on for a truly unconscionable period or you have mistakenly taken poison and are on your way to procure the antidote. It is impolite. Provincetown is an ecosystem, and these street sessions are among its inhabitants' innate characteristics. Displays of impatience or aggressiveness are not considered the badges of personal importance they are in some other places. Anyone in a great hurry is generally perceived not as a mover and shaker but simply as an intruder from a noisier, less interesting world and is likely to be ignored.

Eating and Drinking

PROVINCETOWN IS, OF course, part of New England, a region of hard-knobbed hills and low mountains rising up from a cold ocean amenable only to crustaceans, squid, and some of the hardier, less glamorous finned fish: cods and blues, flounder and bass; fish that tend toward practical shapes, the torpedo or the platter; fish with powerful jaws and blunt, businesslike heads and sleek strong bodies of gunmetal, pewter, or muddy brown. The soil around there produces almost nothing delicate—no fragile or thin-skinned fruits, no tentative greens that would expire in a cold snap, hardly anything that can reasonably be eaten raw. Cranberries and pumpkins do well; bivalves flourish in the chill waters. It is most agreeable to that which has developed thick rinds or shells. If New England has been, from its inception, home to preternaturally determined human settlers, to those who equate hardship with virtue, its Puritan and Calvinist roots are apparent in its diet, which runs not only, of necessity, to that which must have the toughness boiled out of it before it can be served but which tends to eschew, by choice, any spices more flamboyant than salt and pepper. When a friend of mine moved from New Orleans to Boston, she said one night in exasperation, after another bland and sensible meal, "You notice they didn't call it New *France*. You notice they didn't call it New *Italy*."

Fresh fish is Provincetown's most prominent glory, and most fabulous among its fish, to me, are the clams and oysters that come from the tidal flats of Wellfleet, two towns away. A Wellfleet oyster, especially in the colder months, is supernal: firm and immaculately saline, a little mouthful of the Atlantic itself. One autumn several years ago when I was staying for a few days with a friend, she came home in the afternoon with a bucket each of clams and oysters she had dug from the flats in Wellfleet, bearded with bright brown seaweed, and a huge bouquet of wild irises, dark as bruises, with tight, cogent little blossoms so unlike the paler, more ephemeral irises sold in flower shops it was hard to believe they were the same flower at all. It is possible to stride out into the landscape and return not only with dinner but with flowers for the table as well.

Fresh local fish is not, however, as abundant in the restaurants of Provincetown as you might expect it to be. A century or more of excess has depleted the surrounding ocean, and much of what can still be coaxed from the water is bedded in ice and shipped elsewhere. There are only two or three raw bars in town, where you can actually procure shellfish forked out of the sand nearby. Fried clams are easier to find, and while a proper clam roll—crisply fried clams with briny, gelatinous bellies served on a grilled hot dog bun—is a marvelous thing, the precise origins and even the pristine freshness of the clams in question are not matters of great concern. Squid and scallops, among the less endangered inhabitants of these waters, are mysteriously hard to find in restaurants in town, and you're at least as likely to be offered fresh cod in New York or Philadelphia as you are in Provincetown.

To whatever extent a discernible local cuisine exists, it is Portuguese. The Portuguese food most common in New England runs to soups and stews, whatever can be simmered until its fibrousness or bitterness begins to yield. Kale soup studded with circles of linguiça, a Portuguese sausage, is a staple, as are dark, tomato-based squid stews and salt cod in various forms. Some of the local Portuguese families still dry cod in their yards, either laid out flat on the ground or hung from the limbs of trees. But Portuguese food, too, is increasingly hard to find, at least in part because the restaurants of Provincetown have, for some time now, aspired to a certain pan-American sophistication that tends to involve the same pasta and chicken, the same tuna and salmon and beef, that you can get just about anywhere. Generally speaking, you are best advised while in Provincetown to forget any protracted search for indigenous foods and just eat and drink whatever most appeals to you. You need not seek out the rare or quintessential; no one back home will be disappointed if you've failed to taste something famous that's made in a seaside cavern and aged ten years in kelp, or that's been retrieved by specially trained ferrets from the upper branches of particular trees, or that secretes a deadly venom unless harvested at the apogee of the full moon. You are free.

Proof of Gold

You think, living in this town, no one's at war
because of how we all respect savage flowerings
for instance, or the queer biker who walks a stranger
to the curb because the wind is lit up from some strange
cellar to make us late. We think we belong
where we are better known.

I ride my bike. I ride my bike through speeds
like flavors, unzip the mile-long zipper that cinches
the street and sad hay together.
Fletcher named it the Bay of Take What's Left.
But I have seen mornings when all the bay could do
was give nothing but proof of gold
waving. Gold, going on without us.

Michael Klein

Acquisitions

W HEN YOU REACH the middle of town, you
will see, if it is not the dead of winter, that there
is a lot for sale. Like any tourist town, Provincetown needs
you to buy things, many things, so it can live. The human
impulse to shop is, of course, eternal and universal, one of
our identifying characteristics as a species, and I confess to
a queasy but ardent devotion to the search for magical
objects among the gross output of the civilized world. I've
never entirely shed my sense of shame about material-
ism—if I were a true and poetic spirit, if I were the hero
of the story I'd most like to tell about myself, wouldn't I
go to art museums with no thought of the gift shop?—
but have long abandoned hope of transcending my own
urge to search out and acquire. It's hard to know what
to do or say about this endless desire, our collective urge
to feather and refeather our nests, to return bearing the
golden fleece. Here we are (we who are lucky enough), in
our houses, among our things, and for most of us there is

always the tantalizing possibility of something else out there—the shell, the goblet, the golden slipper. Here we are standing before the relics of a saint or the fossilized bones of a mythical monster, moved by the sight and wondering, at the same time, if there may be a postcard or tote bag or snow globe waiting, an addition to our ongoing collection of memento mori; something for us to have.

Provincetown's retail offerings are narrow in one sense (it is difficult to buy a proper hairbrush there, or good stationery, or a pair of dress shoes) and in another sense vast and rich. Treasures abound, though they are hidden among an enormous amount of questionable merchandise. It is as depressingly easy to procure a T-shirt emblazoned with a picture of kittens in bathing suits, a rubber seagull on a string, ugly jewelry, or a "personalized" coffee mug as it is in most beach towns. The town is prone to mysterious retail proclivities that evolve over the years. For quite some time there were a dozen or more shops that sold leather goods—in the business district you were never more than a hundred yards from some place offering an array of leather belts, bags, and jackets. The goods didn't vary much from store to store; each sold variations on the same essential articles: leather knapsacks and cowboy boots; tooled belts with big silver buckles; unsupple, medium-quality leather jackets that never fully shed the smell of their tanning. Over time the leather shops gradually disappeared and have since been replaced by an equally bewildering profusion of stores that sell esoteric household goods. It is now as easy to buy a pair of sporty Italian salt and pepper shakers or a set of wooden sake boxes as it once was to get a black leather jacket with a half-dozen zippered openings. I can only imagine that the customers of Provincetown have matured along with the times and that a certain general fantasy about outlaw status has been replaced by one of stylish domestic prosperity.

Provincetown also boasts several stores so locally vital I feel I should tell you about them in detail. All of the following are, heroically, open year-round, weekdays as well as weekends.

ADAMS PHARMACY

Adams Pharmacy has been in business for over a century and was, until recently, the only drugstore in town. It is full of a sepia-toned version of any drugstore's smell— cosmetics and ointments combined with a subtle odor of powdery cleanliness. It has, over the decades, been half-heartedly modernized. Wood-grain Masonite paneling covers its walls; fluorescent tubes hum on its hundred-year-old wooden ceiling. It is a small hole punched into the present, through which you can see the past—not the preserved, romanticized past of faux general stores and various Ye Olde enterprises but the shaggy genuine article, more than a little dog-eared and moth-eaten, the great-grandmother of the monolithic modern drugstores that abound everywhere in North America. Adams Pharmacy is clean enough and prosperous enough—its shelves are well stocked, it does not reek of decline—but unlike its descendants, with their scoured surfaces and perfect light, it has not shed its sense of our collective meagerness in the face of mortal processes. It is palpably stalwart but puny, and although its pharmacists dispense the same drugs you could get anywhere else, it is more difficult to believe that they will do much good. Adams Pharmacy belongs to a different period in the ongoing history of healing; its roots are not in magical machinery but in artificial limbs, in desperate possibilities ground to dark powders with mortars and pestles, in liquids meant to be poured into handkerchiefs and inhaled by wives with nervous conditions.

The pharmacy's main attraction is its soda fountain, unaltered since at least the mid-1940s. The fountain is staffed by a succession of buxom, semisullen young girls who make a good frappe (the New England term for milkshake). The fountain's cloudy chrome stools are perennially occupied by middle-aged or elderly people who have lived in town most or all of their lives, dressed in finery of their own (a plaid Carhartt jacket, a bright crocheted cap), usually sipping wan coffee from cone-shaped white paper cups set in brown plastic holders. As you walk through the aisles, you can look over and see their faces in the yellowed mirror behind the fountain, under the big old-fashioned Bulova clock with the red second hand big as a conductor's baton, that makes a soft whirring sound as the seconds disappear.

THE A&P

Provincetown has several fine little grocery stores—Angel Foods, on the East End, is particularly good—but in addition to shopping there, I maintain a perverse allegiance to the massive A&P on Shankpainter Road. In the abstract there is nothing good about this store. It was built on wetlands—what was once home to herons and migrating dragonflies is now a parking lot and a big Olde Cape Cod–style strip mall, replete with faux wood siding and faux dormers, that contains a bank, a liquor store, and the A&P. The A&P should, by all rights, be boycotted. I'm slightly ashamed to admit that I go there at least once every time I'm in town.

My devotion stems, in part, from the fact that I live most of the time in New York City, where these gigantic grocery stores are virtually unknown. I shop in corner markets and delicatessens; if it weren't for the A&P in Provincetown, I would have no idea of the number of breakfast cereals produced in America, or of the full range of pork by-products. But more important to me, this standard-issue grocery emporium, being located in Provincetown, is pervaded by a quality I can only call surreal. It is filled, during the summer months, not only with the thriving heterosexual families for whom such a store is intended, but with butches, muscle boys in bathing suits, gay families of various kinds, and the occasional drag queen. Many of the checkout clerks, hired for the summer, check groceries by day and do drag by night. On duty they are brisk and efficient, if more prone to sarcasm than most checkout clerks in most A&Ps. There they stand, every summer, ringing up purchases and putting them in bags, bathed in the fluorescent light—that deeply familiar, shadowless light that fills big stores everywhere; light that is not so much illumination as it is the total obliteration of dark. There they stand, calmly accepting money and making change, ordinary-looking men for the most part, not young, not prosperous, prone to crew cuts and potbellies, with bits of glitter sparking in their hair or on their fingernails, with hints of kohl not quite removed from around their eyes.

MARINE SPECIALTIES

Marine Specialties is a store of such surpassing idiosyncrasy that I can't say, in a simple sentence or two, what exactly it is that it sells. It is a cavern of sorts, something like the genie's cave in the story of Aladdin and the lamp, if by way of treasure the genie had accumulated scented candles (vanilla being especially well represented), laboratory beakers, safari hats, combat boots, ossified starfish, wool sailor's jerseys, vintage pajamas, wind chimes, seconds from the Gap and Banana Republic, rubber balls, Red Cross blankets, pea coats, wool undershirts, camouflage pants, and a hoard of World War II artifacts, up to and including unopened C-rations. It would not be entirely surprising to see stalactites growing from the ceiling toward the back of the shop, dripping on the more elderly merchandise.

Marine Specialties sells more apparel than anything else, but really it just has whatever it has at any given time. It is a repository of the overlooked, the lost, the surplus, the irregular, the no longer needed, and the outmoded. I still wear a pair of orange-and-black-striped pajama bottoms I bought there seven or eight years ago. My friend Dennis owns a glass bottle I bought there for him, prominently labeled HYDROCHLORIC ACID.

Merchandise moves in and out, but some of it takes up what appears to be permanent residence. Certain eccentric parkas, hats, and other items have been there since I first came twenty years ago, still bravely offering themselves for sale. It is hard to find anything that costs more than thirty dollars, and most items are under ten. On the upper, unreachable shelves stands a jumble of random objects (kiddie cars, pennants, piles of ancient hats) and a series of bronze-painted busts of American presidents, the obscure as well as the legendary ones, looking blankly down like carved saints. Marine Specialties is always full of the same light, a brackish yellow-brown, and of the same smell, composed as far as I can tell of mildew, dust, human oils, and an ineffable something I can only describe as age. It is a museum of the disregarded and overlooked; it is the Land That Time *Meant to Have* Forgotten but was not allowed to.

Staying In, Going Out

*P*ROVINCETOWN IS ONE of the better places in the world for staying home at night. Even in summer the nights are rarely warm, and during the rest of the year they range from brisk to life-threatening. Provincetown is particularly amenable to the bed and the book; its houses and inns tend to maintain a properly strict North Atlantic distinction between the inside and the outside. Inside it is warm and well lit. By being inside we provide squares of lamplight, in various off-whites, yellows, and ambers, to shine against the chaos of the night sky, the Canadian winds, the black glitter of the bay. Wanderers on the dark, leaf-tossed roads can look at our lights and take comfort.

At the same time Provincetown is a lascivious carnival during the summer months, and it would be a shame to miss its gaudier pleasures. At night the town is full of the particular spirit of recklessness that obtains in places full of people fully prepared—eager—to do things they would not consider doing at home.

Nightlife in Provincetown is mainly devoted to wandering from bar to bar. Provincetown boasts several grandly disreputable straight bars and considerably more that cater to gay men and lesbians. As far as I know, no men are denied entrance to the women's bars or vice versa. This is Provincetown. Although you would not be popular at the Vault, a leather bar, in Weejuns and a rugby shirt, neither would you be stopped at the door.

Bars in Provincetown not only open and close from season to season but rise and fall in popularity—the hottest bar one summer will be empty the next, only to be hot again the following summer. One, however, is a local institution and will surely be in business as long as Provincetown exists.

THE ATLANTIC HOUSE

The A-House (no one calls it by its full name) has operated steadily, in various forms, since the end of the eighteenth century. It has been a hotel, a restaurant, a cabaret, and a bar, sometimes all four at once, and in more restrictive times was notorious for its lax attitude toward drinking, gambling, and prostitution. Billie Holiday played there for a week toward the end of her life, in the fifties. It is on a narrow side street off Commercial—the newly arrived sometimes have a little difficulty finding it. Look for the street between Vorelli's restaurant and Cape Tip Sports.

The A-House stays open year-round. It is open on snowy winter weeknights in February, and there are always fires in the two fireplaces, even though fewer than a half-dozen people may show up. Although I'm sure the owners are motivated by profit, as any businesspeople are, I consider the A-House's determination to keep its doors constantly open to be a public service.

The A-House has not changed in any way since I went there for the first time more than twenty years ago. It is, has always been, deeply and utterly brown; its atmosphere is full, at all hours, of a crepuscular, sepia-toned dusk. The disco lights on its dance floor create a nimbus of brighter brown; the remoter sections range from coffee to dark chocolate to a shadowy sable-black. The same posters—Sarah Vaughan, Joe Dallesandro in *Trash,* Candy Darling, the Virgin Mary—hang where they have always hung, as do the ropes, cork floats, and lanterns that are the A-House's vague nod to its marine habitat. The Little Bar, on the Commercial Street side, is a leather bar, with a separate entrance. The disco is one door over. The A-House, in both its leather and disco sectors, is musky, its walls and floorboards saturated with the odors of beer and sweat and the soap used to scour beer and sweat away. It is imbued, as older bars tend to be, with sex and disappointment—it is sexy in a damp, well-used way; it occupies a locus where sex, optimism, and disappointment meet. All that desire, much of it fierce or wistful or frustrated, night after night, has insinuated itself as deeply as the smell of spilled beer. You can have a wonderful time at the A-House, but it has always reminded me of Orpheus's descent to search for Eurydice among the shades. It has a furtive aspect, especially as you move away from the dance floor into the deeper darks. This is not entirely disagreeable—why, after all, should the site of so much hope and yearning be cheerful?—but it is unmistakably haunted, the way battlefields are haunted.

In summer, especially on the weekends, the bar is so densely populated by beautiful men, it would be easy to imagine that beauty is the fundamental human state and that you, even if you consider yourself beautiful, have managed to maintain that illusion because you are a fine sturdy goose who has lived long among other geese and only now finds itself in the company of swans. It is not for the faint-hearted, and it is not, I'm sorry to say, full of beauty in its more generous condition, the kind of beauty that includes the beholder, as great courtesans, paintings, and buildings do. It is more the kind of beauty celebrated several hundred years ago in France, when parades involved fully set banquet tables on floats wheeled down the streets with aristocrats consuming lavish dinners on china plates so that the common people could get a glimpse of splendors ordinary invisible to them.

The best times at the A-House are, in my opinion, off season, when most of the other bars in town have closed and everyone in search of anything resembling a party goes there. There are women and men, gay people and straight people. Physical beauty, with all its implied allures and torments, still makes an appearance, but it is rare, as beauty should be, and the people on the dance floor seem generally glad to have been freed from such rampant desire and left to dance in peace.

SPIRITUS

Although the laws in Massachusetts allow bars to stay open until two A.M., Provincetown requires that they close at one, out of consideration for citizens who need their sleep. Many of the people who come in the summertime—gay men in particular—are accustomed to staying out later. At home many don't *leave* for the bars until one A.M., and when the closing lights go on at that hour, there is always a general aspect of shocked disbelief. It is then time for everyone to go up the street to Spiritus.

Spiritus is a converted cottage that sells pizza and ice cream, about five hundred yards west of the A-House. It is open until two in the morning, and when the bars close, everyone goes there, whether or not they have any interest in pizza or ice cream. On summer nights in July and August, literally thousands gather on Commercial Street in front of Spiritus between the hours of one and two A.M. There are vast numbers of men, considerably fewer women. Some men, still sweat-slicked from dancing, mingle with their shirts off; some wear leather chaps with nothing underneath. Some are in drag, and if you're lucky, you might see the Hat Sisters, two ostentatiously mustached gentlemen of a certain age who wear identical drag and make hats for themselves just slightly smaller and considerably more ornate than Christmas trees. The street remains open to traffic—beleaguered cops struggle mightily to clear the crowds away when a car comes through—and if you're foolish or perverse enough to drive on

Commercial Street past Spiritus at that hour, a drag queen or two might very well hop onto the front fender of your car and sing a show tune as you creep along. Please do not discourage this display. You are being blessed.

It's an orgy of sly desire; it's the world's biggest festival for loiterers. It is possible there, if you are a certain kind of person and have lived a certain kind of life, to run into someone you last saw in junior high school in Akron. It is possible to fall suddenly, violently in love, and it is possible to get lucky for the night. It is also possible to have a slice of pizza, talk to an acquaintance or two, and go home to sleep.

That hour at Spiritus is, in a real sense, what the night has been leading up to. Some people, myself included, often skip the bars entirely and go directly to Spiritus at one o'clock. I have been known, on warm nights, to recline on a doorstep across the street from Spiritus with various gaggles of friends, talking and laughing, sometimes with my head in somebody's lap, until we all look up and realize it's almost three and the street is practically deserted.

The crowd starts dispersing when Spiritus closes, but the streets in summer never empty out entirely. Men wander around all night, on foot or on bicycles. Men linger in doorways, sit on the steps of darkened shops, and stroll to and from the dick dock, the stretch of beach behind the Boat Slip hotel, where all sorts of things go on. Late night in Provincetown is, of course, all about sex, but the edginess that prevails in the bars and during the Spiritus hour more or less evaporates. Provincetown after two A.M. is, on the one hand, a small town gone to bed for the night and, on the other, a labyrinth of languid potentiality. Sex settles over the quiet streets like a blanket; it is sexy simply to walk or pedal around, with no intention of bodily engagement, just to watch and listen and to breathe salty nocturnal air so saturated with want. This late, with most of the lights extinguished, more stars are visible, and the foghorn keeps sounding its single note from the break-water. The men who speak to each other do so in low tones that could be mistaken for reverence. A gull wheels by every now and then, very white against the starry sky, and you can hear the soft swish of bicycle tires until just before dawn.

The Want Bone

The tongue of the waves tolled in the earth's bell.
Blue, rippled and soaked in the fire of blue.
The dried mouthbones of a shark in the hot swale
Gaped on nothing but sand on either side.

The bone tasted of nothing and smelled of nothing.
A scalded toothless harp, uncrusted, unstrung.
The joined arcs made the shape of birth and craving
And the welded-open shape kept mouthing O.

Ossified cords held the corners together
In groined spirals like a summer dress.
But where was the limber grin, the gash of pleasure?
Infinitesimal mouths bore it away.

The beach scrubbed and etched and pickled it clean.
But O I love you it sings, my little my country
My food my parent my child I want you my own
My flower my fin my life my lightness my O.

ROBERT PINSKY

Death and Life

*P*ROVINCETOWN HAS BEEN widowed by the AIDS
epidemic. It will never fully recover, though it is
accustomed to loss. Over the centuries men and boys
in uncountable numbers have been swallowed up by the
ocean. Provincetown possesses, has always possessed, a
steady, grieving competence in the face of all that can
happen to people. It watches and waits; it keeps the lights
burning. If you are a man or woman with AIDS there,
someone will always drive you to your doctor's appoint-
ments, get your groceries if you can't get them yourself,
and take care of whatever needs taking care of. Several
years ago the Provincetown AIDS Support Group opened
Foley House, a large house in the East End that has been
converted into apartments for PWAs.

BILLY

Billy was a baker. He was a compact, dark-haired man
with small adroit hands, like an opossum's. He had not

MICHAEL CUNNINGHAM

entirely shed his nasal New Jersey accent, though he
hadn't been back to New Jersey in more than twenty
years. The word *angel,* in Billy's mouth, was "ein-jill" (he
called all his friends "angel"). He lived, as people in
Provincetown do, in a series of apartments, and each time
he moved, he invested his new place with an imper-
turbable, slightly shabby comfort—the effect was roughly
equal parts grandmother and graduate student. There was
always a big dowdy sofa and a few disreputable chairs that,
once you sank into them, were reluctant to let you go,
because they were soft and generous and because they
were exhausted.

Billy was simple, kind, and hospitable, virtues that
count more heavily in Provincetown than they do in
many other places. He and I had been friends for more
than ten years. For my fortieth birthday he made me an
elaborate cake, covered with writing-related decorations:
a miniature television set with a picture of a typewriter
glued onto the screen, pencils interspersed among the
candles. He decided, for obscure reasons, that it should
also include fish, and so he surrounded the cake with
coils of clear plastic tubes full of water and put a half-
dozen live goldfish in them. It should have worked, but
the fish got stuck in the tubes, which traumatized several
of the party guests to the point of tears. The fish survived
the experience, however, and spent the remainder of the
evening in the relative comfort of a mixing bowl.

Billy was my most peculiar and domestic intimate. It
mattered, and sometimes it mattered a great deal, that if

everything collapsed, I knew I could get on a bus, go to Provincetown, and arrive unannounced at his current apartment, wherever it was. Like most people in town, he never locked his door. If it was late, I could have walked in and climbed into bed next to Billy. He'd have half-awakened, and I'd have told him I'd come to live with him for a while. He'd have muttered "Yay" (it was an expression of his), asked no questions unless I wanted him to, and made pancakes the next morning, probably with something exotic and inappropriate in them.

Billy had had AIDS for a long while but was mostly outwardly healthy, if you discount a growing tendency to ramble, which was just an intensified and less cogent version of the way he'd always been. He was carefully watched over by his friends Janice Redman, Michael Landis, and others. Then four years ago he was diagnosed with leukemia. "Are you ready for *this*?" he'd told me over the phone, as if he were imparting an especially scandalous bit of gossip. *"Leukemia. Yikes!"* Neither he nor I knew then that his particular form of leukemia usually proved fatal within a matter of months.

Several weeks later, when I'd gone to Palo Alto to write a story for a magazine, I got a call from Billy's sister telling me he was in a hospital in Boston and was not doing very well. It didn't seem possible—he'd been just fine so recently. I couldn't tell whether his sister, whom I'd never met, was exaggerating, but I decided not to take the chance. I canceled my interview and got on a plane to Boston early the next morning.

By the time I got there, he wasn't coherent. He lay in his hospital bed, moaning and whimpering, surrounded by a half-dozen people. I held his hand and whispered to him. There was no telling whether he knew I was there.

We stayed with him, night and day, in shifts, for the next four days. The day he died there were six of us in attendance: his sister Sue Anne Locascio, Janice Redman, Marie Howe, Nick Flynn, Michael Klein, and me. That last day he moaned and cried out almost continually—we couldn't tell whether he was in pain or having nightmares or both. Toward evening Nick, Michael, and I went out for dinner, and by the time we got back, he had passed away. The three women had been with him. His eyes were still open. His face was blank. The room was full of a silence not quite like other silences: a complete silence, like what it might be like inside a balloon. It seemed that the lights had dimmed, though in fact they had not. After a while, Marie came up to me and said very softly, "I asked the nurse what happens now."

"What happens now?" I asked.

"She said they clean him up and take him downstairs."

"Right."

"I asked her if it would be all right if you three men cleaned him instead. Would you like to?"

I nodded.

I pulled down the blanket and took off his hospital gown. He was still warm, still himself. I closed his eyes. It felt, for a moment, like a melodramatic gesture, something I'd gotten out of the movies and was doing for cheap effect, but it did seem that his eyes should be closed. The lids were soft and yielded easily. I felt the tickle of his eyelashes. Although he had not been in any way frightening when his eyes were open, with his eyes closed he looked less dead. Michael, Nick, and I took warm soapy towels and washed his face and body. There was his pale throat and pale fleshy chest; there were his pink-brown nipples, just bigger than quarters; there was his bush of black pubic hair; and there was his dick, deep pink at the tip, edged in purple, canted at a soft angle to his testicles. We turned him over and washed his back, his ass, and his legs. We turned him over again and pulled the blanket back up.

That was October. We scattered his ashes in January. There was some discussion about where, exactly, his ashes should go. Luanne said he'd told her he had a favorite spot in the dunes, where he'd go to meditate, and Marie and I looked at each other in surprise. As far as we knew, Billy never went into the dunes to meditate. He wasn't fond of sand. We decided he must have said that to his sister to comfort her, to reassure her about his spiritual life.

Nick suggested scattering his ashes in the ocean, but we all agreed that Billy had probably not been entirely certain about just where the ocean was in relation to his living room. It seemed more appropriate to scatter his ashes on the ratty old sofa and turn the television on, but that didn't seem right either. We settled, finally, on the salt marsh at the end of Commercial Street, where the ashes of so many men and women already resided.

The day before the scattering Marie and I went out into the marsh to find a place. It was bitterly cold, with a foot of snow on the ground. We broke, several times, through ice into pools of frigid water. We said to each other, more than once, "This looks good, it's not *too* far from the road, it's sort of pretty if you squint." We periodically shouted, *"Billy,"* in tones that had more to do with exasperation than with grief, which I suspect he'd have appreciated or at least understood. Billy was opposed, in principle, to too much bother in the search for perfection.

We knew immediately, however, when we'd found the place. It was a high dune that appeared to stand almost exactly halfway between town and the water. From there you could see, with equal clarity, the blue-gray line of the ocean and the roofs and windows of town. We stood there awhile, in the frigid silence, on a circle of frozen sand, the sun knifing up off the fields of snow. A scallop boat churned by across the distant snowy dunes. A gull skreeked overhead and dove for something in a pool of slushy gray water. It would soon be time to dismantle Billy's kitchen, to decide what to do about his tables and chairs.

The next day a dozen or so of us carried his ashes out there in his favorite vase, which Janice had made for him, and scattered them on the dune. It was stunningly, stupefyingly cold, the sort of cold that seems to sear all the random particles from the air and render it so pure as to be almost unbreathable. Billy's ashes were creamy gray, studded with chips of yellow-gray bone. When we each took a handful and threw it, some of his ashes lingered in the wind before falling. They did not disappear, as I'd imagined they would. I could see flecks of bone throwing tiny shadows on the sand at our feet. No one delivered a speech or eulogy. It was, to roughly equal extents, solemn and awkward. Some of us had just met. It seemed as if we were waiting for an adult to arrive and tell us what to do. When we were finished, we walked back to town, trying to think of things to say to one another. We got back into our cars, drove to one of the few open restaurants, and had breakfast, as the living do.

Weeks later Marie and I fought over the fact that Billy had, apparently, specifically asked her to carry his ashes when the time came, and I, obsessed with control, determined to be the center of attention, had grabbed them and carried them myself. When we went through his things, a friend of ours, who had scarcely known Billy, was in our opinion far too glad to take one of his belts. This is, as Marie put it, what the living do. We have breakfast with flecks of ash still stuck to our sweaters; we squabble over who behaved insensitively and why.

I go out to Billy's dune every now and then and build something for him. It seems right that he should have an ongoing series of memorials, all of them swept away by wind and water. Once I planted a big stick like a flagpole on top of the dune. Once I found the top of a fence picket, stuck it in the sand like a miniature house, and surrounded it with a fence made of twigs.

Land's End

Provincetown

Zero ground, fickle sandbar
where graves and gravity conspire,

Beer bottle amber and liquor green
surrender their killing shards.

Like ashes, dust, even glass
turns back into what it was.

Skeletal driftwood and seaweed hair
beg for a body. Any body.

Yet all you see is surf out there,
simply more and more of nothing.

If you must leave us, now or later,
the sea will bring you back.

MELVIN DIXON

Where All the Lights Are Bright

A T ITS CENTER, around the entrance to MacMillan Wharf, the town achieves its height of buxom tawdriness. This is the section that most resembles a carnival midway. It is where every store seems to sell the same souvenir T-shirts; where a shop with a prominently displayed saltwater taffy–making machine pumps furiously all day long and into the night. At the intersection of Commercial and Standish streets, where the traffic on a summer afternoon can resemble that in Calcutta, you may be fortunate enough to see a particular traffic cop, a hefty man well into his sixties, who keeps things moving, to whatever extent they can be moved, by means of a whistle, always in his mouth, and a series of pirouettes— he faces traffic in one direction, waves it forward, then abruptly pivots, performs a balletic half turn, stops traffic coming one way, and beckons the others forward. He is like a somber version of the dancing hippos in *Fantasia*.

TOWN HALL

The physical center of town (as opposed to its several different aesthetic, spiritual, and sexual centers) is the block that contains the sedate white bulk of Town Hall. The building houses various municipal offices on its ground floor, which open off a shadowy, dark-paneled hallway hung with time-darkened paintings of Cape Cod. A hush pervades there, always, even at the height of the business day. All activities are conducted behind massive wooden doors fitted with panels of opaque glass. It has always put me in mind of a small-town museum—it wouldn't be surprising to open any of these doors and find not city workers at their desks but glass cases full of stuffed birds, Indian artifacts, and petrified shells.

Up a double flight of wooden stairs, past a mural of fishermen and cranberry pickers, is the auditorium, where town meetings are held. It is also available to anyone who needs to accommodate a large audience. The annual Provincetown AIDS Support Group auction is held there; Karen Finley, Barbara Cook, John Waters, and many others have appeared on its stage.

The auditorium at Town Hall is a big, imperturbably stodgy room, with a bare wood floor and a matronly brown sweep of balcony overhead. It is more classically New England than most of the interiors in Provincetown; more stolid and dim; stingier about comfort. It is sad, anachronistic, and somehow rather grand; a thoroughly indifferent room that seems, even when full, to be empty in its heart; to be waiting patiently for these fools to finish up their business so it can return to its dark, musty contemplation of itself.

The outdoor area in front of Town Hall, however, is far more gregarious. It is lined with wooden benches that were once, years ago, known as the meat rack, where gay men hung around after the bars closed. The benches are now mainly the province of weary tourists and the elderly, whether they are Portuguese women who've raised five children or former bad boys who have gotten too old to dance. In summer you will probably see someone performing for change there: a violinist or folk singer or mime, most likely. One summer a group called the Flying Neutrinos worked the bricks in front of town hall, a ragged group of adults and children (they said they were a family, and might in fact have been) who sang, in a way, and banged on various drums, tambourines, and xylophones. They were the rough local equivalent of Gypsies—they had that quality of treacherous seduction, that sly and defiant otherness. They lived on a houseboat moored off the East End, and all that summer you'd see one or more of them around town, dressed in motley clothes, cheerful if deeply odd, reminding Provincetown that even its people, in all their variety and outlandishness, were still part of a world larger and stranger than any of us can imagine. The next summer they were gone and have not been heard from since. Most recently the bricks were the preferred arena of a man in a clown suit who whistled incessantly and made balloon animals for children, and who was frequently drunk, which inspired him to shout insults at anyone he suspected of being homosexual. Next summer we feel confident that he too will have moved on and been replaced by someone else.

THE MAIN DRAG

The center of town is also the theater district—the place you go to see drag, comedy, and other sorts of shows, at the Post Office Café, Vixen, Tropical Joe's and, back a ways toward the West End, the Universalist church, Town Hall, Antro, and the Crown and Anchor. The acts vary from season to season, but you can rely, every summer, on seeing men perform not only as Judy Garland, Barbra Streisand, Bette Midler, et cetera, but as divas less often seen on the drag circuit, women like Joni Mitchell and Billie Holiday. They generally do their own singing— drag acts have, I'm glad to report, evolved beyond lip-sync. Some, of course, are better than others. I am especially fond of Pearline, who can only be described as a Sherman tank in a wig; Varla Jean Merman, who does a truly filthy rendition of "My Favorite Things" and another number that involves singing while consuming considerable quantities of cheese; and Randy Roberts. Randy is the only one of these people I know personally. Out of drag (or rather in his male drag—as RuPaul once said, "We're born naked, and everything after that is drag") he is a kind, intelligent, unassuming man who lives in Key West in the winters and Provincetown in the summers. In drag he is most visible as Cher, riding up and down Commercial Street to promote his show on a motorized scooter. He is easy to talk to as Randy, somewhat more difficult to talk to as Cher, and I would have to say that I am friendly with one and only acquainted with the other.

Among these artists, but in a category of his own, is Ryan Landry.

RYAN

Ryan has been a local celebrity for over ten years, which, as such things are reckoned there, might as well be a century. He is in his mid-thirties, a tall, dark-haired man with a handsome, equine face and an aspect of sly, wised-up innocence. I want to call him puckish, but he's more substantial than that. Think of the circus performer played by Richard Basehart in Fellini's *La Strada*.

Each summer he produces a show. At first he put on his own versions of Charles Ludlam's versions of *Medea* and *Camille;* then he began writing his own, which have included his takes on *Johnny Guitar, Dracula, Rosemary's Baby,* and Joan of Arc. He is always the star, as he should be. His sensibility falls somewhere between Ionesco and Lucy Ricardo.

He has also, over the years, put on a series of—what to call them?—revues, I suppose. For me, the greatest is Space Pussy, which appears and disappears depending on the summer and is seldom held twice in the same bar or club.

SPACE PUSSY

Space Pussy is presided over by Ryan and the Space Pussy band, which includes a straight man, a gay man, a lesbian, and a transsexual on drums. Anyone who wants to—anyone who gets in touch with Ryan sometime during the week before and agrees to come to one rehearsal—can do a number, but it has to be rock 'n' roll, you have to do your own singing, and you have to wear some sort of drag.

These events are hugely popular, and I try never to miss one when I'm in town. It's wonderful, to me, to witness hoots and applause bestowed lavishly by large crowds on anyone who has the courage to get into costume and mangle "Little Red Corvette" or "Jumpin' Jack Flash" or "White Rabbit" in public. And there is always the possibility of transcendence.

Occasionally someone who has never performed before and cannot, technically, sing at all breaks through to the sublime. The sheer, heady strangeness of it—here I am, in strange clothes, with a good band behind me, delivering a song to an eager audience—can inspire performances of which the person in question is not in any real way capable. I have seen a large, ungainly man, not young, deliver Patti Smith's cover of Van Morrison's "Gloria" with such force, it rattled the ice in my drink. I have heard a woman in girl drag (wigs, gowns, and makeup are, of course, every bit as much drag for some women as they are for men) sing "Ruby Tuesday" with a depth of wrenching melancholy Mick Jagger can only imagine.

Night Song for a Boy

Lock up the church,
I feel as unasleep
as a dead cat: regards
are what I want,
regards, regards, regards.
A priest after boy's ass
feels better than I
do: When I walk around
ladies on the stoops
think I am death: If I
had steel plates on my heels
Oh they would know it.
I should rape a saint
and she could save me
from the dangers of life.

ALAN DUGAN

The East End

AS YOU CONTINUE east, away from the center of
town, you'll notice that your surroundings are
beginning to take on what passes in Provincetown for
staid respectability. The shops on this end generally aspire
to a higher level of dignity. Here you are likelier to find
antiques that are genuine antiques, and jewelry that does
not intend to be whimsical. It is the only part of town
where you could buy a nonsatirical necktie.

The East End is where most of the art galleries are.
Charles Hawthorne taught painting on Miller Hill Road
in the East End, and after his death the studio was taken
over by Hans Hofmann. Franz Kline studied painting with
Henry Hensche in the East End. Mark Rothko bought
a house there in the late fifties, though he didn't live in
it for long. Milton Avery spent summers there in the fifties; Jackson Pollock and Lee Krasner came one summer
before settling in Easthampton. Robert Motherwell summered in his house on the East End for the last forty years

of his life. The East End is where Eugene O'Neill's first plays were produced.

BIG ART, LITTLE ART

The light in Provincetown rivals that of Paris or Venice. Being in Provincetown is like standing on a raft moored fifty miles out to sea. Its light is aquatic; it falls not only down from the sky but up again from the water, so that when you stand there, you do so as if between two immense platters of mirror. Provincetown's shadows are deeper and more complex than the shadows in most other places; its edges are sharper and its colors clearer. If you go there on a sunny day, you may imagine that you've been wearing tinted glasses all your life and have only now taken them off. Painters have been drawn to the light of Provincetown for over a century. Edward Hopper lived in Truro, and his paintings of Cape Cod will give you a good idea of the slightly terrifying purity of the light, its capacity to be exquisite, dazzling, beneficent, and merciless all at the same time. Like most things of great beauty, it is not entirely gentle and not merely pretty, not in any way.

Provincetown has long been a member of that rarefied breed, the artists' colony. Like so many places and people of a certain age, it had a heyday, which can be marked with an unusual degree of precision: As a center for the arts, Provincetown reached its acme in the summer of 1916.

Provincetown's metamorphosis from scrappy little fishing village to artists' colony more or less began in 1873, a year before the first Impressionist exhibition was held in Paris, when railroad lines finally connected Provincetown to Boston. Until then Provincetown had been so difficult to reach that hardly anyone went unless they had business there (which would inevitably have involved whales or fish) or were true adventurers. Provincetown's suddenly increased accessibility was a small part of a titanic shift in the dispersal of people everywhere. In the mid-1800s, railroads in particular and industrialization in general inspired people to abandon rural areas for what seemed at the time like better lives in the cities. Artists, moving in opposition to the larger trends, as artists tend to do, began fleeing the cities to live more cheaply, closer to nature, in the suddenly depopulated countryside. Artists were properly unnerved by the rise of mechanization and what it betokened about the extinction of the handmade, the particular, and the indigenous, which had never before seemed like endangered species. Painters began preferring the regional to the mythic and began leaving their studios to paint outdoors, where they could try and render life as it occurred and light as it fell. With trains—with easier travel across long distances—came the idea of the summer idyll, and rural villages all over Europe and Russia found themselves made into colonies by painters whose ambitions ranged from dabbling to dead seriousness, most of whom arrived determined to find whatever they could of feral and spontaneous beauty; to do justice of one kind or another to the local fields and mountains, the people and animals. At its highest it was the shift in method and intent that spawned the work of Van Gogh, Cézanne, and Monet.

The same current of altered ambition ran through Provincetown, beginning with the railroad, though in Provincetown it all took a somewhat sterner, more New England–ish turn. The seminal event in Provincetown's early life as an artists' mecca was not the sudden appearance of a genius or two but the establishment, in 1899, of the Cape Cod School of Art by Charles Hawthorne, who produced vaguely Manet-like oils of Provincetown scenes and citizens and who was an early American advocate of Impressionism. Hawthorne was a "gentleman painter" who spent his summers in Provincetown and his winters in France and who was generally congratulated for being so unassuming and democratic as to be seen riding a bicycle around town. His Cape Cod School of Art, and several others that started up in Provincetown around the same time, was enormously popular, especially with the wives of wealthy men who began arriving in considerable numbers to spend a summer week or two as bohemians, capped and smocked, laboring at easels set up on the wharves, beaches, and streets.

Provincetown the art colony took a more serious turn with the outbreak of World War I, when artists who might otherwise have gone to Europe found themselves forced to search out some sort of domestic equivalent of the exoticism and low rents their forebears had discovered in Paris. Provincetown naturally suggested itself. And so a new breed of artist—poorer and shaggier, more radical—began turning up on the streets and beaches, elbowing out the matrons and dilettantes.

Eugene O'Neill arrived in the 1910s, as did John Dos Passos, Mabel Dodge, Edmund Wilson, Charles Demuth, Marsden Hartley, Max Bohm, John Reed, and Louise Bryant. They were wild men and women, prone to free love, open marriage, Marxism, psychoanalysis, peyote, and Eastern religion. The women bobbed their hair and eschewed corsets; the men wore berets and open-necked working-class shirts of flannel or corduroy. Charles Demuth sometimes sported a black shirt and purple cummerbund, and Marsden Hartley could be seen in an enormous navy blue coat with a gardenia boutonniere.

They rented the old houses that had once belonged to sea captains. They argued and drank at the A-House and the Old Colony Tap. Everybody slept with everybody. Some of the writers started writing plays, usually about their complicated love affairs, jealousies, and political disagreements. One night in 1915 the writers Neith Boyce and Hutchins Hapgood produced two one-act plays for friends in their home. The first, Boyce's *Constancy*, about the romance between Mabel Dodge and John Reed, was staged on the veranda, with the audience watching from the living room, and the second, *Suppressed Desires*, a spoof of Freudianism by Susan Glaspell and Jig Cook, was put on in reverse, with the audience on the veranda and the play performed in the living room.

They named themselves the Provincetown Players and began staging more elaborate productions in a decrepit

fishing shack on Lewis Wharf that had been bought by
Mary Heaton Vorse, one of the first writers to settle in
among the fishermen of Provincetown. What had been a
lark soon took a more serious turn—the Players realized
that work no one would produce in New York could be
done in Provincetown for little or no money, by and
among themselves. Jig Cook, the leader of the group, had
visions of an American version of the Abbey Players in
Dublin. In what has become locally known as the Great
Summer of 1916, Susan Glaspell said, "We would lie on
the beach and talk about plays—every one writing, or
acting, or producing. Life was all of a piece, work not
separated from play." It was during that summer that
the Provincetown Players put on the first production of
an O'Neill play, *Bound East for Cardiff,* which O'Neill
directed.

☆

EUGENE O'NEILL, THEN twenty-eight years old, the
son of a successful actor, had been sent by his father on a
tramp steamer to Buenos Aires, in the hope that a long
voyage would help cure him of his tendencies to drink
too much and consort with pariahs and derelicts. Young
O'Neill, however, found Buenos Aires more than suffi-
ciently full of alcohol, pariahs, and derelicts, and when
his money and health ran out, he worked his way back
to the United States on a freighter and ended up in
Provincetown.

At twenty-eight he had already begun showing signs of wear; his face had already taken on some of the wounded stateliness he would wear into old age. He dressed as a sailor and did as much as he could to act like one—to eradicate the taint of privilege, to take up a life here in this new place as a rough stranger who'd washed up on the beach, who had never been pampered or cosseted, whose way had never been paid by a father or anyone else. He looked startled and sorrowful and aloof; he might have been a man in the very first stages of transfiguration into an elk. He was not large, but he looked bigger than he was, because he carried himself as if he were large and because he possessed that rare ability to occupy more space than his flesh actually did. Except when drunk, he was taciturn and vaguely disapproving; people who knew him then tended to love and fear him to roughly equal extents, and many believed—or hoped—that he harbored for them some special affection that he was unable or unwilling to demonstrate by the conventional means. Women adored him.

Bound East for Cardiff, which concerns a dying seaman named Yank on a ship bound for North America from Argentina, was performed at Lewis Wharf on a foggy night in the summer of 1916, with the water of the incoming tide splashing audibly under the floorboards. It was revelatory. Those who attended the performance that night discovered what the larger world would learn soon enough: that even in his early efforts O'Neill was a transforming agent in American theater. He insisted on an

American version of the grim, resolutely unflorid work of European playwrights like Strindberg and Ibsen, whom he admired; he was the first American to write about lower-class life in lower-class language, without condescension or cheap attempts at moral uplift.

O'Neill lived in Provincetown for eight years in various places, among them a room over the A-House. He wandered the streets in seaman's clothes, in a riot of melancholy drunkenness. He had a tortured affair with Louise Bryant. He made Abbie Putnam, the strict and rather terrifying local librarian, into a character who murders her child in *Desire Under the Elms*. Eventually he married a woman named Agnes Boulton and settled with her in the Peaked Hill Life-Saving Station, a grand old barn of a building on the edge of the Atlantic that could be reached only by a half-mile hike through the dunes. (It has since collapsed into the ocean.) It had been renovated by Mabel Dodge, who painted the walls white and the floors blue and furnished it with antiques brought back from Europe. O'Neill wrote nineteen short plays and seven long ones in Provincetown, most of them while he lived in the house at Peaked Hill. He taught himself how to write during that time and had at his disposal a body of amateur actors and set designers who would mount everything he wrote. He became a great artist there, in what he called "a solitude where I lived with myself." He was at home at Peaked Hill when he learned, from a neighbor, that he had won the 1920 Pulitzer Prize, the first of his four Pulitzers. He celebrated quietly, with his wife, in their capacious and remote house, with its blue floors and its two couches that had been bought by Mabel Dodge from the estate of Isadora Duncan.

FURTHER ART, OTHER ART

After World War I ended, after the preeminence of European painting and sculpture was toppled by the work of American artists, Provincetown's remoteness turned fairly abruptly from its central virtue to its most prominent liability. Who wanted to live so far from New York City, when New York had become the center of the world? A few artists spent their summers there, Robert Motherwell prominent among them, but Provincetown had become a backwater, a retreat, and many of the famous names connected with the town—people like Milton Avery, Mark Rothko, Jackson Pollock, and Lee Krasner—were there only a summer or two. Still, a body of serious painters and sculptors like Paul Bowen, Fritz Bultman, Nanno de Groot, Chaim Gross, Peter Hutchinson, Karl Knaths, Leo Manso, Jack Tworkov, and Tony Vevers all lived there during the second half of the twentieth century, and some of them live there still.

Since the 1940s progressive little galleries have opened, thrived, and ultimately closed: Forum 49 and Gallery 256 and HCE (for "Here Comes Everybody," from Joyce's *Finnegans Wake*); the Sun Gallery, which in 1959 showed Red Grooms's *Walking Man,* possibly the first installation (known at the time as a "happening") to involve live actors; and the Chrysler Museum, where Andy Warhol and the Velvet Underground put on *Exploding Plastic Inevitable*.

By the late 1960s, however, Provincetown had devolved into a straightforward tourist town, albeit one with a slightly higher incidence of foment and creation than most other places whose main occupation was being visited. All the edgy little galleries had gone out of business, and the people who emigrated there were likelier to be seeking peace and quiet than inspiration, agitation, or argument. Those who went to the A-House and the Old Colony Tap went only to drink.

In 1969 Stanley Kunitz, Robert Motherwell, and other artists and writers who were upset about Provincetown's decline set out, essentially, to restock the town with younger artists and writers the way a forest service restocks a lake with fingerling trout. They raised a modest sum of money and bought Days Lumber, a defunct lumberyard on the East End. They converted it into studios, which they offered to artists and writers, along with a small but livable monthly allowance, and called it the Fine Arts Work Center in Provincetown. It is still there.

The buildings of the Work Center, on Pearl Street, are agreeably disorderly. They include the long flat-roofed buildings that were once Days Lumber, a shingled barn that has been made over into studios, and two cottages fading among the weeds. Among the writers, painters, and sculptors who have received fellowships early in their careers, lived for a while in Provincetown, and gone on to more visible careers are Richard Baker, Maria Flook,

Nick Flynn, Ellen Gallagher, Louise Gluck, Marie Howe, Denis Johnson, Tama Janowitz, Yusef Komunyakaa, Jhumpa Lahiri, Jenny Livingston, Elizabeth McCracken, Sam Messer, Ann Patchett, Jayne Anne Phillips, Jack Pierson, Louise Rafkin, Kate Wheeler, Jacqueline Woodson, and Lisa Yuskavage.

Due partly to the Fine Arts Work Center, and partly to the increasingly imponderable cost of living in New York City, Provincetown has to a certain extent been revived as an art colony. Still, it is not what it once was. Provincetown today is something like an elderly bohemian who once knew people of great influence, who still dresses eccentrically, still lives in defiant poverty, still paints or sculpts with heroic optimism, and flirts only on bad days with bitterness about having been gifted and dedicated and having been left behind.

As far as literature is concerned, O'Neill remains the town's great-grandfather, its most venerable ghost. Tennessee Williams summered there in the forties—he stayed at Captain Jack's Wharf, on the West End—but as far as I can tell, none of the more hopeful rumors about his relationship to Provincetown are true. He did not write *The Glass Menagerie* or anything else there; he did not seduce the young Marlon Brando there, as a condition for getting him the lead in *Streetcar*. He came, it seems, for the same reasons so many have—for the sun, the quiet, and the boys.

The poets Mark Doty and Mary Oliver live in Provincetown today, and Stanley Kunitz spends each spring and summer in his house on the West End. Norman Mailer lives year-round in a big brick fortress of a house on the East End. Alan Dugan lives just over the line, in North Truro.

ALTHOUGH FEW OF the visual artists living and working in Provincetown are internationally known, some of them are in fact very, very good. On the one hand, Provincetown offers every form of artistic travesty, from landscapes and seascapes painted on assembly lines in Korea to dreadfully earnest Impressionist-style paintings of sunlit gardens and village streets. But on the other, it shows and sells work that is much edgier, work that engages the world in more complicated ways, that takes in not only the beauty of the skin but the existence of the skull beneath. I am looking, right now, at a shadowy charcoal drawing of a nocturnal Provincetown street by John Dowd, which I keep close by for inspiration when I write, along with a miniature lamp sewn into a square of white silk organza by Melanie Braverman; a series of mysteriously compelling random snapshots by Sal Randolph; a great cartoonish painting of an empty stage by Polly Burnell; a haunting photograph of a cottage by Marian Roth; and two little ceramic houses by Pasquale Natale that speak to equal extents of comfort and menace.

The painters, photographers, and sculptors of Provincetown need to sell their work as urgently as any artists do, but because the scale is so much smaller and the market so much broader, they are free to do whatever they feel moved to do, without the obligation to Be Important or to Move Art Along. Beauty as a subject in itself doesn't sell very well in the larger world these days—you'd be hard pressed to find a serious gallery in New York or Los Angeles or another big city showing many newer artists whose work isn't ironic, defiantly ugly (if *defiant* is the right word for such relative unanimity), and intended as commentary on the state of the culture at large. These are lean years for young still-life and portrait painters. A frank love of the visible world and a determination to pay tribute to it won't get you very far just now. But you can do fine in Provincetown.

What passes for a dowager on the Provincetown art scene is the Provincetown Art Association, a gracious, rambling old white building in the East End with a trove of work by the luminaries and semiluminaries of Provincetown past and present. The galleries of Provincetown are not averse to showing work that aspires unashamedly to the rendering of the visible world, but at the same time some of them also show the work of artists who might be a little too far out there for most galleries in New York. Provincetown is where Kathe Izzo can get permission to live for several days in a gallery and arrange herself as a living tableau. It is where Michelle Weinberg could make a gown in the shape of a giant pink While You Were Out slip for opera singer Debbie Karpel, who wore it and stood in the window of a gallery on Halloween night, singing arias. It is where Sal Randolph could, last October, curate a show of free art, in which dozens of artists from town participated and at which you could take anything you wanted, as much as you wanted, for free.

THE FAR EAST END

As you walk past the stores and galleries of the East End, your most dicey aesthetic interlude will occur as you pass a four-story hotel that spans both sides of Commercial Street, a minor monument to ordinariness, with its sad little swimming pool surrounded by a cyclone fence. This place is known, locally, as the green monster, though it is no longer green. Directions are often given in terms of whether the place in question stands before (east) or after (west) the green monster. When it went up over thirty years ago, the selectmen quickly passed legislation forbidding any further structures more than two stories tall.

East of the green monster you are on solid sightseeing ground. You will walk for about another half-mile past the houses that line the bay, the best of which are dreams. They are old and slightly precarious, as houses on water often are. In calamitous weather, they would be the first to go. They are not generally much ornamented; they are sensible New England houses, content with their salt-weathered shingles, their shutters and porches and dormers. They eschew fancy moldings and woodwork. There is not a cupola among them. Wooden houses (only one, Norman Mailer's, is made of brick) subjected to this much weather are built like boats, with a bit of sway—the fact that they move slightly in strong winds is part of what keeps them standing. You can see through some of them; that is, you can look into a streetside window and see the bay through a rear window, like a living painting the owners have hung, one in which clouds shift and gulls glide by. The houses on the water in the East End, standing as they do on their sandy strip between asphalt and salt water, are not only dreams but are dreaming. With the exception of an occasional newcomer stuck in among them, they have been here long. Some of the children who played in summers on these porches eventually died of old age in one of the upstairs bedrooms. The houses here are not just unusually vulnerable to weather and tides. They are prone to an extra degree of ephemerality, as if one or two of them might, after all this time, forget that it was a house at all and simply dissolve into the bay.

HELLO HELLO HELLO

Several summers ago my friends Marie Howe and James Shannon lived in a cottage on the East End. At the end of their block, two weather-beaten houses faced each other across the street. A pair of elderly women lived in one of the houses. They were always inside, always watching television, wrapped in blankets. They ate their meals from trays in front of the TV.

Two old men lived in the opposite house. We could see, through their windows, that their house was full of what I would call junk but what they, surely, considered their holdings. Their living room was full of old radios and television sets, among other things, none of which appeared to work. One of the men, who might have been eighty, sat every day in the scrap of yard before his house on a dirty white plastic chair that had conformed itself to the shape of his body. He did not hear very well, or at all—it was difficult to determine. Every time anyone passed his house, he would smile, nod, and shout, "Hello hello hello," in a cracked but resonant voice. James, Marie, and I agreed that when we grew old and infirm, if we were lucky enough to live that long, we would not be the sort of old people who huddled all day in front of a television set. We would be the sort of old people who set up chairs outside and yelled "Hello hello hello" to everyone who passed.

THE END OF THE EAST END

Eventually you'll reach the forked intersection of Commercial and Bradford streets. The town line is a short distance away. Ahead of you is the long, languid stretch of Beach Point, with its gaggle of waterfront motels and cottages. Beach Point is lovely, in its corrupted way. Most of the motels date back to the forties and fifties, long one-story wooden buildings that tend to sport modest neon signs involving seagulls and to offer each guest a pair of metal lawn chairs, rusty at their edges, their backs molded in the shape of scallop shells. At the far eastern end, well beyond your range of vision here, across the Province-town line, there's a line of beach cabins, twenty or more, white, perfectly identical, with the precise shape and proportions of the houses in the Monopoly game. A sign on each of them proclaims that it is named after a particular flower: rose, daisy, zinnia, marigold, hollyhock.

We, however, will stop here. Stand for a minute or two just east of the last waterfront house, where the bay splashes right up to the foot of the road. To the east, ahead, is a small harbor within the harbor, formed by the jut of Beach Point. If it's high tide, you'll see a body of calm water giving back the sky. If it's low tide, you'll see an expanse of wet sand, still bearing the ridges made by the subsided water. The sand will be modestly hillocked, shaped as it is by currents, so that in the lower parts oblongs and parabolas of clear salt water shine. If the weather's warm, the sand will be full of the people staying at the motels on Beach Point, and a good number of them will be children. The elderly may sit in folding chairs they've brought out with them. The younger adults, parents of the children, will be watching their children and looking out at the water, one hand raised to shield their eyes. The children will be running around, digging in the sand or kicking at it, splashing in the pools, heeding or ignoring their parents' admonishments not to go too far, not to abuse their brothers or sisters, not to make quite so much noise. People have been doing exactly this, in just this way, for the last two hundred years.

Now

Whatever the foghorns are
the voices of feels terrible
tonight, just terrible, and here
by the window that looks out
on the waters but is blind, I
have been sleeping,
but I am awake now.
In the night I watch
how the little lights
of boats come out
to us and are lost again
in the fog wallowing on the sea:
it is as if in that absence not many
but a single light gestures
and diminishes like meaning
through speech, negligently
adance to the calling
of the foghorns like the one
note they lend from voice
to voice. And so does my life tremble,
and when I turn from the window
and from the sea's grief, the room
fills with a dark

lushness and foliage nobody
will ever be plucked from,
and the feelings I have
must never be given speech.
Darkness, my name is Denis Johnson,
and I am almost ready to
confess it is not some awful
misunderstanding that has carried
me here, my arms full of the ghosts
of flowers, to kneel at your feet;
almost ready to see
how at each turning I chose
this way, this place and this verging
of ocean on earth with the horns claiming
I can keep on if only I step
where I cannot breathe. My coat
is leprosy and my dagger
is a lie, must I
shed them? Do I have
to end my life in order
to begin? Music, you are light.
Agony, you are only what tips
me from moment to moment, light
to light and word to word,
and I am here at the waters
because in this space between spaces
where nothing speaks,
I am what it says.

DENIS JOHNSON

The Water

*I*F YOU GO to Provincetown and spend all your time
there on land, you cannot properly claim to have seen
the place, any more than you could claim to have seen
New Mexico if you went to Santa Fe and didn't stray
beyond the city limits. In Provincetown it is possible to
imagine the Atlantic as a backdrop, there to provide shimmer and wind as a foil for all this commerce. Once you
are a half-mile or less from shore, however, you understand that Provincetown and everything in it is actually a
minor, if obstreperous and brightly lit, interruption in the
ocean's immense, inscrutable life.

MACMILLAN WHARF

In the exact middle of town is the entrance to MacMillan
Wharf. This is where train tracks once ran right out onto
the end of the wharf; where trains arrived empty and left
loaded with whale oil, whalebone, and baleen. It is one
of the half-dozen surviving wharves—there were once

about sixty—and it still functions as it was meant to, though it's nothing like what it was in its prime. Fishing boats still dock there, and some of what the fishermen are able to pull from the depleted waters is processed on the wharf.

The wharf is immense, by local standards. Underneath, amid the brown trunks of its pilings, which are covered with mussels and scraps of seaweed, it nurtures a swatch of permanent shade. On top it is, essentially, a wide asphalt road that extends well out into the water. Cars and trucks come and go at all hours. The wharf smells of fish, as you would expect it to, but its fish smell is layered. The fresh and briny covers something fetid, not just dead fish but old oil and machinery that has been overheated again and again and again. From the side of the wharf, you can see fish swimming in water that is the color of deep, cloudy jade—just minnows usually, though you might see a bass or a bluefish dart by. The *Hindu* docks there, an eighty-year-old schooner that takes tourists on two-hour sails. The whale-watching boats dock there, too.

Fishing is among the most dangerous of professions—the mortality rate among fishermen is almost ten times that among firefighters and policemen. This may account for the somber aspect that attaches to MacMillan Wharf, for all its tourist enticements. The wharf is subtly but discernibly haunted, a midway zone between the gaudy comforts of town and the shimmering immensity beyond. At the far end is a small village of trailers for processing fish, the harbormaster's bungalow, and the Pirate Ship *Whydah* Museum, devoted to the treasure-laden ship of Captain Kidd, which sank in the waters off Wellfleet. All around them are the masts and lines of the small, privately owned fishing boats, the names of which tend to be either affectionate or wistful: the *Chico Jess,* the *Joan Tom,* the *Second Effort,* and the *Blue Skies.*

The fishing boats, when you see them up close from the wharf, are battered and faded, thoroughly marked by their rough use. Scallop boats go out for weeks at a time, in all weathers. Their decks are usually littered with plastic buckets, cork floats, and disorderly piles of rope and net, most of which have aged to a smoky chestnut color. It's clear that the ocean and its weather turn that which was once white to gray or yellow, that which was once bright to chalk, and that which was once dark to brownish-black. What there is of color usually resides in a fisherman's pair of new orange waders, or a shroud of new fishnet, white or green, that has not yet begun to blacken.

Walk out to the end of the wharf. Scavenging gulls will be making their usual racket. Men who have been darkened by the ocean will be working on the boats or standing in small groups, talking and drinking coffee from paper cups. From the end of the wharf you can get a closer look at the breakwater where the foghorn blows at night; you can see that all along its top it is a pearly, variegated white from seagull shit, which in that quantity is slightly phosphorescent. You can look farther out to Long Point, past the pleasure boats anchored in the bay. You can look back and see the long parabolic curve of the town and the ocean. It is the best way, while still on land, to understand how graceful and small the town must look, how touchingly inconsequential, to whales as they breach, farther out.

I'm especially fond of walking to the end of MacMillan Wharf late at night, when it's nearly empty. If you go there then, you will hear the boats creaking against the pilings. You will see the hard white light of the harbormaster's office. The water will be full of gulls, calmer now that the fish are stored away, white as beacons as they swim along over the dim watery gray of their paddling feet. At the end of the wharf a brilliant blue Pepsi vending machine will shine against the black water and the starry black sky.

Fish

Most of the commercial fishing around Provincetown is done now by enormous corporate-owned boats, with auditorium-sized refrigerators, that can go far out into less-depleted waters and stay there until they've caught their limit. There are still tuna out there, in deep water, though they too are largely the quarry of big-money fishermen with expensive gear. A large tuna—they grow to eight feet and can weigh twelve hundred pounds—might bring as much as twenty thousand dollars; in summer several representatives of Japanese companies install themselves at MacMillan Wharf, ready to buy the choicest parts of the best tuna and overnight it to Japan. Every now and then a local hero takes one from a small boat, but it's a job of Hemingway-esque proportions. A full-grown tuna is likely to be bigger than your boat. Once you've hooked it, you have to shoot it in the head, the way they shoot cattle in slaughterhouses, then lash it to the side of your boat and head back for shore. This happens rarely.

For all intents and purposes, only a few fish worth noticing remain close to the shores of Provincetown. There are, as I've said, scallops and squid and lobsters. There are flounders and what are known as trash fish—goosefish and dogfish and wolffish. And there are game fish.

The waters around Provincetown are full of bass and bluefish, which you can catch from the beach or a small boat. Blues are the criminals of the ocean. They are, essentially, sets of teeth that swim. When they're running, in late August and early September, you can stand on the beach and see patches of roiling water, as close as twenty feet out, which occasionally manifest a flash of silver. This is a school of bluefish devouring a school of minnows. Catching blues involves a slightly perverse devotion to battle. Pulling one into your boat is something like being in a small room with an angry pit bull, and if you do win the fight, what you've got is a dark-fleshed, oily fish suitable only for grilling or smoking. Grilled bluefish can be a fine thing, but nobody prizes bluefish, no one hungers for it, no restaurant offers it as a signature dish.

Bluefish will eat anything. They will strike at a length of broom handle, painted white, with a hook at its end. James told me he once pulled a blue into his boat and fought so hard with it that one of its eyes was gouged out before the fish struggled back into the ocean, half blind. James, ever practical, used the disembodied eye as bait and almost immediately caught the same fish again, which had struck at its own eye on a hook.

Bass are another matter entirely. Bass are regal and lithe, calm the way athletes are calm, with athletes' coiled, slumbering ferocity. Almost anyone can hook a bluefish (though not just anyone can land one); to hook bass you have to know what you're doing. A bass is, essentially, a tunnel with a mouth at one end. They suck their food straight in without swallowing, so that if one takes your bait and you pull too soon, the bait and hook will just pop back out and the bass will swim away, barely traumatized. When a bass strikes, you've got to wait until the right moment and jerk the line in just the right way, so your hook buries itself in the fish's stomach. Then the fight begins.

Bass are present but not plentiful, so the taking of them is strictly regulated. Fishermen are allowed one per day, and it must be at least thirty inches long. No fisherman with any conscience would think of violating those rules. James often hooks a bass that proves to be too small, or he keeps catching them after he's caught his limit, just for the love of it, though he always throws those fish back. Once the fish is in the boat, however, before throwing it back, he does something he tells me is customary among people who love to fish. He kisses it.

WHALES

A hundred and fifty years ago the waters around Provincetown were so full of whales, it was possible to harpoon them from shore. The front yards of most houses sported, as lawn ornaments, whale jaws and whale ribs, often bedecked with morning glories. If a pod of whales ventured close to shore, whalers jumped into their boats and herded them onto the beach. Shebnah Rich wrote of one such melee in his book, *History of Truro:*

> *The vast school of sea monsters, maddened by frantic shouts and splashing oars, rushed wildly on the shore, throwing themselves clean onto the beach; others pursuing, piled their massive, slippery carcasses on the first, like cakes of ice pushed up by the tide, till the shore presented a living causeway of over six hundred shining mammals, the largest number at that time ever driven on shore in one school. They landed at Great Hollow. The news reached the church just at the close of the morning service. During the next few days while the stripping was going on, thousands came to the circus. Some who had never seen such an aquatic display were wild with delight, jumping from fish to fish and falling among them as among little mountains of India rubber.*

The surviving whales now live, largely unmolested, some distance out to sea. We who once killed them as recklessly and rampantly as pioneers killed off the buffalo of the prairies can pay to get on boats that will take us out to see them.

For years I resisted going out on the whale-watching boats. It felt unseemly, even grotesque, an intrusion on the privacy of creatures who ought better to be left alone. I could not imagine standing on the deck of a whale-watching boat without feeling like someone Diane Arbus would have been all too glad to photograph.

I was wrong. The whale-watching excursions are miraculous, and I urge anyone who feels reluctant for any reason to simply get on a boat and go. While I've tried to shy away from promoting any one local enterprise over another except when it seems absolutely necessary, I should tell you that the Dolphin fleet is the one operated by the Center for Coastal Studies, which uses the profits to fund its ongoing study of the migratory and other habits of whales.

The trip takes about four hours, and much of that time involves churning your way across empty water to get to the places where the whales feed. Whales are migratory—they winter to the south and come north in summer. You are most likely to see humpbacks, which are barnacle-bearded creatures, snouted, with broad black-gray backs and pale gray bellies. Their mouths (like most whales, they eat plankton) are gigantic hinges set high in their heads, and their eyes, surprisingly small, are set far back and low, close to their mouths. You may also see pilot whales or schools of dolphin. I should warn you that from day to day and summer to summer the whales are capricious in their choices of feeding grounds. They are always out there, but some summers they are too far away for the boats to get to where they are and back within four hours, and some days they seem simply to have decided to be in a place where the boats are not. Whale watches are gambles. You might see no more than a distant breaching or two; you might return having witnessed nothing beyond a distant almond shape, expelling a miniature spray of water. I have been on a fruitless trip during which, after hours of sailing around and seeing nothing, a middle-aged woman stood at the prow of the boat, wearing a pantsuit and holding a straw clutch decorated with straw strawberries, and said, "Ooh, come on, you finky whales." The leviathans did not respond.

On a good day, however, you will see them come to within feet of the boat, and it is one of the more remarkable things that can happen to a human being. The whales don't seem to mind the boats—if anything, they seem mildly curious about them, the way a land-living creature might wonder about a rock or a tree it could swear hadn't been there yesterday. They are docile but not in any way bovine. They are, of course, immense, though you don't comprehend that fully until you've seen one up close. They are benign, enormously powerful, and unconcerned with us. They are, at close range, utterly fleshly. Their slick backs are scarred and notched; the flesh of their underbellies is scored with pliant-looking ridges you could sink your whole hand into. Their heads and bodies are sometimes freckled and dappled like an Appaloosa's hindquarters.

Being mammals, they are not entirely hairless. Their eyes have short, bristly lashes. They snort and sigh and exhale; they expel jets of water through their blowholes, which form spangles of iridescent mist over their backs. They smell powerfully of fish and of themselves, a smell like that of fish but oilier, deeper, so potently rank, you suspect it may linger in your clothes and hair.

If you're very fortunate, you may see a whale jump straight up from the water, three-quarters of its length, and crash down again. A whale when it jumps is, momentarily, aloft, suspended: all that tonnage, all that blubber, though the word *blubber* is hard to apply to such sleek and muscular beings. If you see one jump, you will understand how perfectly built they are (you who were never really meant to walk upright), how much like living torpedoes. There is nothing about them that does not speak directly to their ability to swim. Their flukes are enormous, gracefully curved, broad and flat, covered with barnacles. Their mouths, meant to scoop up vast quantities of plankton, constitute almost a third of their bodies; their heads in profile are wedges that terminate in the broad hard-rubber rims of their mouths, which meet in an overlap, like the lid of a box.

The whales don't jump often, at least not for the benefit of whale-watching boats. They are more prone to breaching, their heads underwater, showing their scarred, glistening backs as they take in oxygen through their blowholes. After a minute or two they dive again. Their backs disappear underwater, and a moment later, as they angle themselves to dive, they flip their two-pronged black tails up from amid the chaos of churn and foam they've created.

I once stood at the rail and watched a humpback swim under the boat, no more than twenty feet down, so we could see its whole body, so we could fully understand how buoyant it was and begin to understand that it truly occupied the water. The whale was deep green in the green-blue water, shadowy as an X-ray, netted with pallid light. The sight was stirring and somewhat frightening, not because the whale could or would damage the boat but because it was revealed, briefly, in its realm, the vastness that lay under us, with its schools of darting fish; its granular, sun-filtered green that would deepen by slow degrees to jade, lusterless emerald, and then pure black; its submerged cliffs and plains and valleys where, among the fissures, darker fish swam over a bare, porous landscape of rock without needing to see; where pinpoints of luminescence drifted and anemones waved their translucent petals.

Epilogue

ENNY AND I met in Provincetown over fifteen
years ago. I was living in Brooklyn then and had
gone up for the weekend with my friend Bob Applegarth
(whose ashes we scattered several years later on the big
dune at the end of Snail Road). Kenny, who lived in
Manhattan, was in Provincetown for a week by himself,
though he was not often by himself once he got there. We
spoke to each other casually, as strangers do, in an art
gallery, then ran into each other again, later that night in
front of Spiritus, where we exchanged phone numbers. If
we hadn't happened onto each other that second time, I
suspect we'd never have met again, and we've wondered
over the years whether we were likely ever to have met,
under any circumstances, in New York. It seems doubtful.
We had little, outwardly, in common. But Provincetown
is the kind of place where people who are not technically
supposed to meet at all not only do so but see one another
over and over again. Kenny and I have been together all of

the last fifteen years, and we still go to Provincetown every chance we get. We imagine ourselves, only half jokingly, as old coots there, prone to a little more gold jewelry than is absolutely necessary, walking wire-haired dachshunds on leashes down Commercial Street. I can think of worse fates. Wherever you go, Provincetown will always take you back, at whatever age and in whatever condition. Because time moves somewhat differently there, it is possible to return after ten years or more and run into an acquaintance, on Commercial or at the A&P, who will ask mildly, as if he'd seen you the day before yesterday, what you've been doing with yourself. The streets of Province-town are not in any way threatening, at least not to those with an appetite for the full range of human passions. If you grow deaf and blind and lame in Provincetown, some younger person with a civic conscience will wheel you wherever you need to go; if you die there, the marshes and dunes are ready to receive your ashes. While you're alive and healthy, for as long as it lasts, the golden hands of the clock tower at Town Hall will note each hour with an electric bell as we below, on our purchase of land, buy or sell, paint or write or fish for bass, or trade gossip on the post office steps. The old bayfront houses will go on dreaming, at least until the emptiness between their boards proves more durable than the boards themselves. The sands will continue their slow devouring of the forests that were the Pilgrims' first sight of North America, where man, as Fitzgerald put it, "must have held his breath in the presence of this continent, compelled into an aesthetic

contemplation he neither understood nor desired, face to
face for the last time in history with something commen-
surate to his capacity for wonder." The ghost of Dorothy
Bradford will walk the ocean floor off Herring Cove,
draped in seaweed, surrounded by the fleeting silver lights
of fish, and the ghost of Guglielmo Marconi will tap out
his messages to those even longer dead than he. The
whales will breach and loll in their offshore world, dive
deep into black canyons, and swim south when the time
comes. Herons will browse the tidal pools; crabs with blue
claws tipped in scarlet will scramble sideways over their
own shadows. At sunset the dunes will take on their pink-
orange light, and just after sunset the boats will go lumi-
nous in the harbor. Ashes of the dead, bits of their bones,
will mingle with the sand in the salt marsh, and wind
and water will further disperse the scraps of wood, shell,
and rope I've used for Billy's various memorials. After
dark the raccoons and opossums will start on their rounds;
the skunks will rouse from their burrows and head into
town. In summer music will rise up. The old man with
the portable organ will play for passing change in front of
the public library. People in finery will sing the anthems
of vanished goddesses; people who are still trying to live
by fishing will pump quarters into jukeboxes that play
the songs of their high school days. As night progresses,
people in diminishing numbers will wander the streets
(where whaling captains and their wives once prome-
naded, where O'Neill strode in drunken furies, where
Radio Girl—who knows where she is now?—announced

the news), hoping for surprises or just hoping for what the night can be counted on to provide, always, in any weather: the smell of water and its sound; the little houses standing square against immensities of ocean and sky; and the shapes of gulls gliding overhead, white as bone china, searching from their high silence for whatever they might be able to eat down there among the dunes and marshes, the black rooftops, the little lights tossing on the water as the tides move out or in.

Acknowledgments

If space permitted, it would be appropriate to thank everyone who lives in or loves Provincetown. I must, however, limit myself to the people who read this book in manuscript, and helped me with the prose and the facts. I extend my particular thanks to Mark Adams, Janet Biehl, Ken Corbett, Melanie Braverman, Mary DeAngelis, Dennis Dermody, John Dowd, Marie Howe, Anne Lord, Mark McCauslin, Molly Perdue, Sal Randolph, Marian Roth, Ellen Rousseau, and James Shannon.

I also relied on the Pilgrim Monument and Provincetown Museum for information about Provincetown's past, and am particularly grateful to Jeffory Morris, the curator there. I also referred to *Provincetown as a Stage* by Leona Rust Egan, *Time and the Town* by Mary Heaton Vorse, and Tony Vevers's essays in the catalog of the Permanent Collection of the Provincetown Art Association and Museum.

Doug Pepper, my editor, was a writer's dream come true. And I am always indebted to Gail Hochman, Meg Giles, and Marianne Merola.

Credits